Prayer Keys

Prayer Keys

Clift & Kathleen Richards

Victory House, Inc.
Tulsa, Oklahoma

Prayer Keys
Copyright © 2001 by K. & C. International, Inc.
ISBN 0-932081-74-6 (Mass-market Paperback)
Published by Victory House, Inc.
P.O. Box 700238
Tulsa, Oklahoma 74170
(918) 747-5009

CONTENTS

Introduction

ACKNOWLEDGMENTS

The authors wish to acknowledge the capable assistance of their editor, Lloyd Hildebrand, and the staff at Victory House for their hard work, encouragement, and insightful contributions.

Books of Interest from Victory House

Introduction

Prayer is the soul's sincere desire,
Uttered or unexpressed;
The motion of a hidden fire
That trembles in the breast.
(William A. Schulthes)

We begin our Christian walk with prayer as we invite our Lord Jesus Christ to come into our hearts, forgiving us of our sins and cleansing us from all unrighteousness. (See Rom. 10:9-10 and 1 John 1:9.) Then, as we study His Word and stand upon His promises, we are able to pray with understanding according to the will of God. (See 1 John 5:14-15.)

The Christian walk has been compared to a wheel that has Christ Jesus at its hub, for truly He is the center of everything in a believer's life. Emanating from the center of the wheel are four strong spokes that keep the wheel straight as it rolls along life's road. One of those important spokes is the Bible – God's Word to us. (See Heb. 4:12.) Truly, it is a road map for our Christian journey.

A second important spoke is Christian fellowship. As we associate with like-minded believers, we learn to become more accountable for our actions, and more responsible toward God and others. This is why church attendance is so important for every child of God. As we pray with and for others we are strengthened spiritually. (See Heb. 10:25.)

The third spoke of the wheel of life is witnessing. God guides us to people who need to know Him. He loves everyone, and as we share His love with others, many will come to know Him and to serve Him. What a glorious privilege it is for every believer to lead others to Jesus Christ. (See Acts 1:8.)

The fourth strong spoke of the wheel is prayer. Prayer is a major avenue of blessing in our lives. It opens doors for us to walk through and windows of understanding that help us to see things more clearly. Prayer enables us to remain in intimate and vital contact with God, our heavenly Father. (See Matt. 6:6.)

The Christian's wheel of life is lubricated with the oil of the Holy Spirit. It is balanced with love. It is propelled by faith. No matter how bumpy the road becomes, the wheel keeps going on. Though it might wobble a bit from time to time, it is never thrown off track because its direction and purpose are set to be always straightforward, and its transmission is in high gear.

Prayer maintains the wheel, and the purpose of this book is to help us to understand major components of prayer – *Prayer Keys* – which empower us to pray more effectively. The Bible says that the effective, fervent prayer of a righteous person avails much. (See James 5:16.)

Prayer Keys provides us with fifteen keys to effective prayer. Everyone knows that a key is a useful instrument. Most keys are metal instruments that enable us to turn the bolt of a lock or start a vehicle. The function of a key is to gain or prevent entrance, possession, or control. These definitions of a key denote its real and actual purposes.

Often, the word *key* is also used as a metaphor for understanding, identification, and explanation. In this usage, the word *key* can mean a clue that enables one to solve a problem. As we examine keys to effective praying, we will see how important and useful prayer is in all that we say, think, and do. We will gain insights into the dynamics of prayer and the steps to answered prayer. We will discover the power of believing prayer.

Believing prayer gives us access to the glorious throne room of God. "Let us therefore come boldly to the throne of grace, that we may obtain mercy and find grace to help in time of need" (Heb. 4:16, NKJV). It opens the door to everything God has in store for us.

Believing prayer also closes the door to all unwanted visitors and intruders. It keeps the devil and his workers at bay. It locks out all temptation and every form of evil.

Believing prayer has the quality of spiritual authority which enables us to take command of every situation. It also enables us to take possession of the promises of God. "For all the promises of God in Him are Yes, and in Him Amen, to the glory of God through us" (2 Cor. 1:20, NKJV).

No wonder we are commanded to: "Rejoice always, pray without ceasing, in everything give thanks; for this is the will of God in Christ Jesus for you" (1 Thess. 5:16-18, NKJV).

The great Victorian poet — Alfred, Lord Tennyson — knew these truths about prayer. He wrote:

> *More things are wrought by prayer*
> *Than this world dreams of.*
> *Wherefore, let thy voice*
> *Rise like a fountain . . .night and day.*

God has given us the great spiritual resource of prayer. As Tennyson points out, the world has no idea of the power of God that is available through believing prayer.

This vital resource is the Father's way of access and blessing in His kingdom

As you study and use *Prayer Keys*, may God ". . .give to you the spirit of wisdom and revelation in the knowledge of Him, the eyes of your understanding being enlightened; that you may know what is the hope of His calling, what are the riches of the glory of His inheritance in the saints, and what is the exceeding greatness of His power toward us who believe, according to the working of His mighty power which He worked in Christ when He raised Him from the dead and seated Him at His right hand in the heavenly places, far above all principality and power and might and dominion, and every name that is named, not only in this age but also in that which is to come" (Eph. 1:17-21, NKJV).

KEY # 1 – PRAY ACCORDING TO THE WILL OF GOD

Now this is the confidence that we have in Him, that if we ask anything according to His will, He hears us. And if we know that He hears us, whatever we ask, we know that we have the petitions that we have asked of Him.
(1 John 5:14-15, NKJV)

Confidence in God

It is confidence in God that leads us to pray in the first place. Confidence involves both faith and trust. For the believer, these qualities come by way of the holy Scriptures. Paul wrote, "So then faith comes by hearing, and hearing by the word of God" (Rom. 10:17, NKJV).

Likewise, confidence is assurance – assurance that God will always honor His Word to us. Confidence in God is an assurance that He loves us and always knows what's best for us. It is an assurance that He knows what we need, even before we express it to Him. (See Matt. 6:8.) It is an assurance that He hears and answers our prayers (when we pray according to His will).

It is confidence in God that causes us to believe the promises of His Word which proclaim to us that "All things are possible to him that believeth" (Mark 9:23). Confidence in God helps us to know this truth: "I can do all things through Christ which strengtheneth me" (Phil. 4:13). Confidence in God removes all fear and enables us to pray effectively, as the Bible commands: "Lift up thy voice with strength; lift it up, be not afraid" (Isa. 40:9).

Perhaps the best definition of confidence in God is found in the book of Proverbs where we read: "Trust in the Lord with all your heart, and lean not on your own understanding; in all your ways acknowledge Him, and He shall direct your paths" (Prov. 3:5-6, NKJV). Confidence, therefore, is abiding trust.

Ask According to His Will

In teaching His disciples how to pray, Jesus prayed, "Thy will be done in earth, as it is in heaven" (Matt. 6:9-10 and Luke 11:2). God's will is the most important thing on earth, and in our individual lives. That's why Jesus prayed, "Not my will, but Thine, be done" (Luke 22:42 and Mark 14:36) in the Garden of Gethsemane on the night of His betrayal.

"The world passeth away, and the lust thereof: but he that doeth the will of God abideth for ever" (1 John 2:17). Prayer is an integral part of God's will for our lives. The

Bible clearly states, "Rejoice always, pray without ceasing, in everything give thanks; for this is the will of God in Christ Jesus for you" (1 Thess. 5:16-18, NKJV).

God's will is revealed to us in His Word. He wants us to pray without ceasing, for clearly this is His will for us. He also wants us to rejoice always and to give thanks, because these elements of prayer are crucial in the believer's life.

Jesus said, "Ask, and it shall be given you; seek, and ye shall find; knock, and it shall be opened unto you" (Matt. 7:7). Faith that God will answer your prayers is cultivated through adherence to biblical principles that will not fail. Praying according to the will of God (as it is revealed in His Word) brings us everything God wants us to have. This form of praying is prayer that is rooted in the confidence that God hears us and that He wants to answer us.

E.M. Bounds wrote, "To know God's will in prayer, we must be filled with God's Spirit, who makes intercession for the saints according to the will of God. To be filled with God's Spirit, to be filled with God's Word, is to know God's will." (From *The Necessity of Prayer* by E.M. Bounds.)

Familiarity with the Word of God, and praying from a scriptural perspective, always produces phenomenal changes both in our praying and our living. It affects all that we say, think, and do. Praying according to the will and Word of God calls His power into action, unleashing the Holy Spirit to move in our behalf.

It has been said that prayer changes things. Prayer according to the will of God always changes things because God's power is a dynamic force in our lives, continually bringing forth change and growth. Most importantly, praying according to the will of God enables us to *accept* the will of God, even if His will is sometimes different from what we may have originally hoped. Jesus said, "If ye abide in me, and my words abide in you, ye shall ask what ye will, and it shall be done unto you" (John 15:7).

Allowing the words of God to find their place within our hearts puts our minds in accord with the will of God. Then, as we pray His Word and His will, our will becomes one with His. It is in conforming our will to the Father's (through the operation of the Spirit and the Word in our lives) that we know our prayers will be answered.

E.M. Bounds wrote, "Such filling of the heart with the Word and the Spirit gives us an insight into the will of the Father. It enables us to rightly discern His will and puts a disposition of mind and heart within us to make it [God's Word] the guide and purpose of our lives." (From *The Necessity of Prayer* by E.M. Bounds.)

We know God's will through His Word and His Spirit. The Bible tells us that God wants us to train our children properly so that they will be able to find the right paths for their lives, "Train up a child in the way he should go, and when he is old he will not depart from it" (Prov. 22:6, NKJV). The truth of this Scripture has been proven time and again in the lives of parents and children throughout the ages.

One key component to effective parenting is prayer. The mother of John and Charles Wesley, Susanna, had nineteen children. Her faithful practice was to spend at least one hour per week with each of her children separately, listening to them, praying for them, and teaching God's Word to them. Susanna's prayers, like those of the woman who bore her name in the Gospel of Luke, were based on love for the Lord and faith in His Word.

Susanna claimed the promises of God in behalf of her children, and He heard and answered her earnest pleas. John Wesley became the most famous leader of the Evangelical movement in the British Isles, the founder of Methodism. His brother, Charles, composed great hymns of the Church that are sung throughout the world.

Susanna Wesley prayed according to the Word of God. She prayed the will of God, and He fulfilled His promises to her by leading her children in the paths of righteousness, and He has done the same for our children as well.

As parents, we have discovered that prayer is one of our greatest resources. As we've prayed for our children when they've faced difficult circumstances, God has always intervened. In addition, He has given us greater wisdom to help us know how we can best help our children. God is our faithful Father, and His parenting in our lives has helped us to become better parents.

God Hears Us

It would be an empty exercise to pray without believing that God is listening to us. He does hear us. In fact, He is always waiting for us to come to Him in prayer. On the day when the Lord had delivered David from the hand of all his enemies, the great leader of Israel affirmed: "The Lord is my rock and my fortress and my deliverer; the God of my strength, in whom I will trust. . . .I will call upon the Lord, who is worthy to be praised; so shall I be saved from my enemies. . . .In my distress I called upon the Lord, and cried out to my God; *He heard my voice from His temple, and my cry entered His ears"* (2 Sam. 22:2-7, NKJV).

Notice what happened next: "The earth shook and trembled; the foundations of heaven were shaken, . . .The Lord thundered from heaven, and the Most High uttered His voice. He sent out arrows and scattered them; lightning bolts, and He vanquished them . . . .He delivered me from my strong enemy, from those who hated me; for they were too strong for me. They confronted me in the day of my calamity, but the Lord was my support. He also brought me out into a broad place; He delivered me because He delighted in me" (2 Sam. 22:8-20, NKJV).

God took delight in David's prayer. He heard Him, and He took action in His behalf. As a result of David's prayer according to God's will, the Lord God became David's defender, leading David to proclaim, "For You are my lamp, O Lord; the Lord shall enlighten my darkness. For by You I can run against a troop; by my God I can leap over a wall. As for God, His way is perfect; the word of the Lord is proven; He is a shield to all who trust in Him" (2 Sam. 22:29-31, NKJV).

Yes, God hears us when we pray. When Hezekiah was sick unto death the prophet Isaiah reminded him that God hears and answers prayer: "Thus says the Lord, the God of David your father: 'I have heard your prayer, I have seen your tears; surely I will heal you'" (2 Kings 20:5, NKJV). God heard the prayer of Hezekiah, and He saw his tears. He answered him by healing him and giving him fifteen more years of life.

God "heareth the cry of the afflicted" (Job 34:28). The Psalmist knew this truth when he wrote, "The Lord will hear when I call unto Him" (Ps. 4:3), and "He forgetteth not the cry of the humble" (Ps. 9:12). In fact, the Book of Psalms is filled with truths about God's ever-listening ear:

"Blessed be the Lord, because He hath heard the voice of my supplications" (Ps. 28:6).

"I sought the Lord, and He heard me, and delivered me from all my fears" (Ps. 34:4).

"The righteous cry, and the Lord heareth" (Ps. 34:17).

"Call upon Me in the day of trouble: I will deliver thee, and thou shalt glorify Me" (Ps. 50:15).

"As for me, I will call upon God; and the Lord shall save me" (Ps. 55:16).

"He shall call upon Me, and I will answer him: I will be with him in trouble" (Ps. 91:15).

"Because He hath inclined His ear unto me, therefore will I call upon Him as long as I live" (Ps. 116:2).

"In my distress I cried unto the Lord, and He heard me" (Ps. 120:1).

"The Lord is nigh unto all them that call upon Him, to all that call upon Him in truth" (Ps. 145:18).

These mighty prayer promises are echoed in the Book of Proverbs as well: "The Lord is far from the wicked: but He heareth the prayer of the righteous" (Prov. 15:29).

One of the greatest affirmations of the fact that God hears us when we pray was penned by the prophet Jeremiah: "Call unto Me, and I will answer thee" (Jer. 33:3).

Does God hear us when we pray? Every promise of the Bible responds with a resounding YES, because we know, "The eyes of the Lord are over the righteous, and His ears are open unto their prayers" (1 Pet. 3:12).

God is speaking; are you listening? God is listening; are you praying? He will hear and answer your prayers.

We Know We Have the
Petitions We Have Asked of Him

As we pray according to God's will and Word, believing that He hears us as we pray, we then have the full assurance that He will grant our petitions. The Bible says, "Whatsoever we ask, we receive of Him, because we keep His commandments" (1 John 3:22).

A petition is a formal request that is made to one in authority. It involves something of great importance to us. When Jonah found himself in the belly of a giant fish there was really only one thing that he could do which might lead to his deliverance, and that one thing was prayer. Through prayer, he put forth his petition to the Father even though he knew that he had been disobedient to God.

Jonah turned back to God in the midst of his calamity: "I cried by reason of mine affliction unto the Lord, and He heard me; out of the belly of hell cried I, and Thou heardst my voice. . . .And the Lord spake unto the fish, and it vomited out Jonah upon the dry land" (Jon. 2:2,10). It was prayer that brought God's aid to His unfaithful servant. Through the force of this prayer of desperation, Jonah was set free from "the belly of hell" to serve God as he had been called to do.

E.M. Bounds writes, "Just as God has commanded us to pray always, to pray everywhere, and to pray in everything, so He will answer always, everywhere and in everything. God has plainly and with directness committed Himself to answer prayer. If we fulfill the conditions of prayer, the answer is bound to come. The laws of nature are not so invariable and so inexorable as the promised answer to prayer." (From *The Possibilities of Prayer* by E.M. Bounds.)

Truly the possibilities of prayer are endless. God tells us that He will grant our petitions when we pray according to His will. This is the Father's promise to us.

God's Word gives us a multitude of examples of people who prayed according to God's will and received direct and mighty answers:

"For this child I prayed; and the Lord hath given me my petition" (Hannah, in 1 Sam. 1:27).

"He did hear my voice out of His temple, and my cry did enter into His ears" (David, in 2 Sam. 22:7).

"He heareth the cry of the afflicted" (Elihu, in Job 34:28).

"The Lord will hear when I call unto Him" (David, in Ps. 4:3).

"Blessed be the Lord, because He hath heard the voice of my supplications" (David, in Ps. 28:6).

"Because He hath inclined His ear unto me, therefore will I call upon Him as long as I live" (David, in Ps. 116:2).

"Seek ye the Lord while He may be found, call ye upon Him while He is near" (Isaiah, in Isa. 55:6).

"Thou hast heard my voice: hide not Thine ear" (Jeremiah, in Lam. 3:56).

"We do not present our supplications before Thee for our righteousnesses, but for Thy great mercies" (Daniel, in Dan. 9:18).

"Whosoever shall call on the name of the Lord shall be delivered" (Joel, in Joel 2:32).

"Your Father knoweth what things ye have need of, before ye ask Him" (Jesus, in Matt. 6:8).

"Every one that asketh receiveth" (Jesus, in Matt. 7:8).

"Whatsoever ye shall ask in prayer, believing, ye shall receive" (Jesus, in Matt. 21:22).

"Whatsoever ye shall ask in my name, that will I do, that the Father may be glorified in the Son" (Jesus, in John 14:13).

"The same Lord over all is rich unto all that call upon Him" (Paul, in Rom. 10:12).

"By prayer and supplication with thanksgiving let your requests be made known unto God" (Paul, in Phil. 4:6).

"Ask in faith, nothing wavering" (James, in James 1:6).

"The effectual fervent prayer of a righteous man availeth much" (James, in James 5:16).

"The eyes of the Lord are over the righteous, and His ears are open unto their prayers" (Peter, in 1 Pet. 3:12).

"Whatsoever we ask, we receive of Him, because we keep His commandments" (John, in 1 John 3:22).

These precious prayer promises from God's Word give us confidence in praying. They reveal God's will to us. They show us that God hears us when we pray according to His Word. The knowledge that He does, in fact, hear us assures us that He will grant our petitions because we know He loves us.

Andrew Murray writes, "The more heartily we enter into the mind of our blessed Lord, simply thinking about prayer as He thought, the more surely His words will become living seeds. They will grow and produce their fruit in us – a life corresponding exactly to the Divine truth they contain. Do let us believe this: Christ, the living Word of God, gives, in His words, a Divine quickening power which brings what they say, which works in us what He asks, and which actually enables us to do everything He demands." (From *The Ministry of Intercession* by Andrew Murray.)

Our first prayer key is praying according to the will of God. This involves confidence, trust, assurance, and faith – qualities that are imparted to us through the Word of God. (See Rom. 10:17.) As we pray according to His will, we soon discover that God is actually listening to our prayer, and because we know He is listening and that He loves all of His children, we are assured that we will receive the petitions we've put before Him.

Praying according to the will of God is an important key to receiving all that we really need from Him. He cares about us, and He wants to supply all of our needs. Paul wrote, "And my God shall supply all your need according to His riches in glory by Christ Jesus" (Phil. 4:19, NKJV).

Prayer of Application

Heavenly Father, I delight to do your will. O my God, your Word is within my heart.[1] Teach me how to pray according to your blessed Word and will[2] as I lift my voice to you.[3]

Thank you for revealing your will to me, Father, through the Scriptures and the life of your Son. You have poured out your Spirit upon me and you have promised to make your words known unto me.[4]

Your Word is quick and powerful. Indeed, it is sharper than any two-edged sword. Your glorious Word pierces even to the dividing asunder of my soul and spirit, and it is a discerner of my thoughts and the intentions of my heart.[5]

Thank you for your Word, Father. It truly is a light unto my path and a lamp unto my feet.[6] With your help I will walk in your Word and I will honor your Word as I pray. I resolve, dear Father, to never let your Word depart from my mouth. I will meditate upon its truths all day long, and I will prevail in prayer as I pray your Word. As this becomes a reality in my life, I know you will make my way prosperous and you will fill my life with success.[7] Thank you, almighty God.

Throughout my life you have performed your Word over and over again.[8] You have confirmed it to me in so many ways. It is my delight to hide your Word in my heart so that I will not sin against you.[9]

Father, your way is perfect and your Word is tried. You are a mighty shield to me, and to all who trust in you.[10] How I thank you for the realization that your Word will accomplish all that you please in my life.[11]

Father, I want to become a doer of your Word at all times, including when I pray. I do not want to be a hearer of your Word only, but I also want to be a pray-er of your Word.[12] By keeping your Word as I live and pray, I know your love will be made perfect in me. Give me the grace, Lord God, to be a doer, pray-er, and keeper of your Word at all times.[13] Thank you, Father.

References: (1) Psalms 40:8; (2) 1 John 5:14-15; (3) Psalms 3:4; (4) Proverbs 1:23; (5) Hebrews 4:12; (6) Psalms 119:105; (7) Joshua 1:8; (8) 1 Kings 8:20; (9) Psalms 119:9-11; (10) Psalms 18:30; (11) Isaiah 55:10-11; (12) James 1:22; (13) 1 John 2:5.

REMEMBER THIS: PRAY ACCORDING TO THE WILL AND WORD OF GOD. GOD PROMISES TO HEAR AND ANSWER YOU WHEN YOU DO.

2

KEY # 2 – PRAY IN THE NAME OF JESUS

*Most assuredly, I say to you, whatever
you ask the Father in My name He will give
you. Until now you have asked nothing
in My name. Ask, and you will
receive, that your joy may be full.*
(John 16:23-24, NKJV)

The Name Above Every Name

The name of Jesus is above every name.
(See Phil. 2:9.) His is a name that rings with
authority, and the very mention of His name
brings peace to the troubled heart. Paul wrote,
"Therefore God also has highly exalted Him
[Jesus] and given Him the name which is
above every name, that at the name of Jesus
every knee should bow, of those in heaven,
and of those on earth, and of those under the
earth, and that every tongue should confess
that Jesus Christ is Lord, to the glory of the
Father" (Phil. 2:9-11, NKJV).

Yes, the name of Jesus stands for all the
power and authority of Almighty God. In fact,
Jesus said, "All authority has been given to
Me in heaven and on earth" (Matt. 28:18,
NKJV). Because this is true, when we pray in

the name of Jesus we are calling His power and authority into action on our behalf. This power even causes demons to flee and every knee to bow. The highly exalted name of Jesus represents supreme authority, and praying in His name brings glory to the Father.

Jesus is seated at the Father's right hand, far above all principalities and powers, and ". . .every name that is named, not in this age but also in that which is to come" (Eph. 1:21, NKJV).

Because Jesus is with the Father now, we are able to avail ourselves of His divine power through prayer. Jesus promises us, "Most assuredly, I say to you, He who believes in Me, the works that I do he will do also; and greater works than these will he do, because I go to My Father. And whatever you ask in My name, that will I do, that the Father may be glorified in the Son" (John 14:12-13, NKJV).

We see the truth of this promise revealed when Peter and John ministered to the lame man who laid at the temple gate. Peter said to him, "Silver and gold I do not have, but what I do have I give you: In the name of Jesus Christ of Nazareth, rise up and walk" (Acts 3:6, NKJV). In "the Name above every name" the disciples were able to do the healing work of Jesus, and the man's feet and ankles were strengthened, enabling him to walk and leap.

The people were amazed at this miracle, and Peter told them, "And His [Jesus'] name, through faith in His name, has made this man strong" (Acts 3:16, NKJV). Truly, the name of Jesus is above every name, and faith in His name brings dynamic power to our prayers.

Jesus, Our High Priest

Prayer unleashes the power of God into any given situation. Jesus said this is possible because He goes to the Father. This works in two ways: First, Jesus goes to the Father in prayer for us. "Therefore He is also able to save to the uttermost those who come to God through Him, since *He always lives to make intercession for them*" (Heb. 7:25, NKJV). Jesus lives to make intercession for us!

Knowing this helps us to go to God with confidence and expectation. Jesus is our High Priest who prays for us. "Seeing then that we have a great High Priest who has passed through the heavens, Jesus the Son of God, let us hold fast our confession. For we do not have a High Priest who cannot sympathize with our weaknesses, but was in all points tempted as we are, yet without sin. Let us therefore come boldly to the throne of grace, that we may obtain mercy and find grace to help in time of need" (Heb. 4:14-16, NKJV).

Jesus, our High Priest, knows all about us. He understands every situation we face. He sympathizes with us. He prays for us.

Secondly, Jesus went to the Father after His death, burial, resurrection, and ascension. Now He is seated at the right hand of God, the Father. He said, "Nevertheless I tell you the truth. It is to your advantage that I go away; for if I do not go away, the Helper will not come to you; but if I depart, I will send Him to you" (John 16:7, NKJV). This passage shows us how it is possible for us to do everything He asks us to do. He has sent the Holy Spirit (our Helper) to continue His work in us and through us.

It is through prayer and the power of the Holy Spirit that we are enabled to do great things for God, and to experience the fullness of His joy.

Whatever You Ask in Jesus' Name

"In Jesus' name" is a phrase that is frequently attached to prayer as a complimentary close, much like one might close a letter with "Yours truly" or some similar expression. Although this is certainly an appropriate practice, it does not come close to the meaning Jesus wanted us to understand when He told us to pray in His name.

In effect, He was giving us the power of attorney to represent Him – and all of His interests and everything He possesses – by praying in His name. To pray in the name of Jesus, therefore, is to pray in the full realization of who He is, what He stands for, what He is able to do, and what He wants. We are representing Him when we are praying in His name, and so we must be sure that our prayers are in agreement with Him.

He pointed this out to His disciples: "Abide in Me, and I in you. . . .If you abide in Me, and My words abide in you, you will ask what you desire, and it shall be done for you" (John 15:4-7, NKJV).

What an exciting privilege it is to know that we can pray with His authority as it is represented by His name. At the mention of His name (when spoken in faith), the demons have to flee, and every knee shall bow when His name is uttered.

Andrew Murray wrote, "He [the Lord Jesus] longed so much for us to really believe that His Name is the power in which every knee should bow, and in which every prayer could be heard, that he did not weary of saying it over and over: 'In My name.' Between the wonderful *whatsoever ye shall ask, and the Divine I will do it, the Father will give it,* the simple link is: 'In My name.' Our asking and the Father's giving are equal in the Name of Christ. Everything in prayer depends upon our comprehending this: 'In My name.'" (From *The Ministry of Intercession* by Andrew Murray.)

A friend of ours named Brian had been raised in a godly home. His parents had prayed for him daily. As a youth, he had held promise as a good musician. Unfortunately, however, he made several wrong choices in his adolescence and adulthood, and he became an alcoholic – a man without money, friends, home, family, or purpose.

One Sunday morning he awoke on a park bench in a northeastern city of the United States. A verse that his parents had taught him came to his mind: "Nor is there salvation in any other, for there is no other name under heaven given among men by which we must be saved" (Acts 4:12, NKJV). It was a verse that his parents (now deceased) had taught him when he was just a boy. That name, Brian knew, is *Jesus,* and it leaped into his heart with a force like a thunderbolt. "It's the name of Jesus," Brian said to himself over and over again.

He began to whisper, "Jesus, Jesus, Jesus . . . ." It was like a mighty wave began to build deep within his soul, and he began to experience something that he had not felt for many years. It was joy surging deep within.

As excitement began to build within his heart, Brian heard church bells chiming. The compelling sound came from a little white church with a steeple, which he spied just across the courtyard. He later reported that he felt literally drawn to that church. The name of Jesus and the joy of anticipation continued to swirl within his heart as he headed toward the little Baptist church.

Though unkempt, Brian entered the sanctuary. He didn't notice the stares he received from the ushers and certain members of the congregation. All he saw was the picture of Jesus over the altar. "Jesus," he prayed. "Change my life."

The minister came out and announced, "You have read my sermon text and title for this week, but just a few moments ago I felt led to change them. This morning I want to speak to you from Acts 4:12 – there is no other name under heaven given among men by which we must be saved." As the pastor held forth the name of Jesus, the convicting power of the Holy Spirit fell upon Brian, and he knew that God loved him. The minister gave an altar call, and Brian went forward, surrendering his heart and life to the One whose name truly is above every name. He prayed, in the name of Jesus, and his life was totally transformed in an instant!

The prayers Brian's parents had prayed decades before had now borne fruit. God reached down and saved a disillusioned, disheveled man, and this same man went on to become a Christian musician and a leader in helping others find freedom from alcoholism and drug addiction. Brian now says, "The power in the name of Jesus set me completely free. I'm a new man. My life has meaning and purpose I never knew before."

If You Ask Anything in Jesus' Name, He Will Do It

At least six times in the gospels Jesus reiterated the importance of praying in His name. He gave us the legal right to use His name in prayer because He chose us to be His representatives on earth. He wants us to fulfill His Great Commission: "Go therefore and make disciples of all the nations, baptizing them in the name of the Father and of the Son and of the Holy Spirit, teaching them to observe all things that I have commanded you; and lo, I am with you always, even to the end of the age. Amen" (Matt. 28:19-20, NKJV).

One of the things Jesus commanded us to do is to pray in His name. He assures us that He will be with us always. He said, "I have chosen you. . . .that whatsoever ye shall ask of the Father in my name, He may give it you"

(John 15:16). One of the reasons why Jesus chose us was so that we would learn to pray in His name. Through this means the Father's will shall be accomplished on earth.

Jesus wants us to have joy, and this is another reason why He wants us to pray in His name. He said, "Verily, verily, I say unto you, Whatsoever ye shall ask the Father in my name, He will give it you. Hitherto have ye asked nothing in my name; ask, and ye shall receive, that your joy may be full" (John 16:23-24).

Clearly, God's power is unleashed in the believer's life when he or she uses the name of Jesus in full realization of who He is, what He has accomplished, and what He is doing and will do. Through the proper use of His name in prayer, we will accomplish great works, the Father will be glorified, and we will experience unspeakable joy. The joy comes from the fact that we know we will receive what we ask when we pray in Jesus' name.

Who Jesus Is

The Scriptures show us how powerful and important the name of Jesus actually is, and they reveal who He is to us:

"His name shall be called Wonderful, Counsellor, The mighty God, The everlasting Father, The Prince of Peace" (Isa. 9:6).

"They shall call His name Emmanuel [God with us]" (Matt 1:23).

"His name was called JESUS" (Luke 2:21).

"At the name of Jesus every knee should bow" (Phil. 2:10).

Truly, the name of Jesus is the most wonderful name ever given. The Bible gives us great insights into the power, authority, and glory of that mighty name as it shows us that Jesus is:

"The Lamb of God" (John 1:29).
"The Son of God" (John 1:34).
"The Messiah" (John 1:41).
"The Son of man" (John 1:51).
"The bread of life" (John 6:35).
"The light of the world" (John 8:12).
"The door" (John 10:9).
"The Good Shepherd" (John 10:11).
"The way, the truth, and the life"
    (John 14:6).
"The true vine" (John 15:1).
"The King of the Jews" (John 19:19).
"The Holy One and the Just" (Acts 3:14).
"The Deliverer" (Rom. 11:26).
"That great shepherd of the sheep"
    (Heb. 13:20).
"The Judge" (James 5:9).
"The chief Shepherd" (1 Pet. 5:4).
"The true light" (1 John 2:8).

"The faithful witness" (Rev. 1:5).

"The prince of the kings of the earth" (Rev. 1:5).

"The morning star" (Rev. 2:28).

"The Word of God" (Rev. 19:13).

"The King of Kings, and Lord of lords" (Rev. 19:16).

"Alpha and Omega" (Rev. 22:13).

"The beginning and the end" (Rev. 22:13).

"The first and the last" (Rev. 22:13).

All of these titles that are given to Jesus in the Bible reveal His attributes and qualities to us. They speak of His power, authority, and radiance. When we pray in His name, therefore, we are operating in His power and authority.

Paul wrote, "Let the word of Christ dwell in you richly in all wisdom; teaching and admonishing one another in psalms and hymns and spiritual songs, singing with grace in your hearts to the Lord. And whatsoever ye do in word or deed, do all in the name of the Lord Jesus, giving thanks to God and the Father by him" (Col. 3:16-17).

We are admonished to do everything in the name of Jesus, including prayer. This inevitably brings great results and helps us to become fruitful in all that we do.

Jesus said, "Ye have not chosen me, but I have chosen you, and ordained you, that ye should go and bring forth fruit, and that your fruit should remain: that whatsoever ye shall ask of the Father in my name, he may give it to you" (John 15:16).

We did not choose Jesus; He chose us! One of the main reasons why He chose us was so that we could bring forth fruit in His name. When we pray in His name, God takes action in our behalf and we become fruitful Christians who know how to bear lasting fruit.

Another wonderful prayer promise comes to us from the lips of Jesus: "Again I say unto you, That if two of you shall agree on earth as touching any thing that they shall ask, it shall be done for them of my Father which is in heaven. For where two or three are gathered together in my name, there am I in the midst of them" (Matt. 18:19-20).

All of this is possible when we pray in the name of Jesus. "And these signs shall follow them that believe; In my name shall they cast out devils" (Mark 16:17). The power and authority inherent in the name of Jesus conquers all the forces of darkness.

I love the name of Him whose heart
Knows all my griefs and bears a part
Who bids all anxious fears depart

I love the name of Jesus.
Jesus, oh how sweet the name!
Jesus, every day the same;
Jesus, let all saints proclaim
Its worthy praise forever.
(Edmund S. Lorenz)

Prayer of Application

Heavenly Father, I come to you in the mighty name of Jesus,[1] because I know the power of His name works wonders in my life and the lives of others. Without Jesus I can't accomplish anything of lasting value, including prayer;[2] therefore, I commit myself to prayer in His name and authority.[3]

Thank you, Father, for showing me that I can do all things through Christ Jesus because He strengthens me.[4] He is the King of kings and the Lord of lords,[5] and I rejoice in the wonderful realization that He is the way, the truth, and the life[6] for me in prayer and in all aspects of my life.

In Jesus I have wisdom, sanctification, righteousness, redemption,[7] and answered prayer.[8] How I thank you, Father, that you gave your only begotten Son to be my Savior,[9] and thank you for letting me be crucified with Him. Because I have been crucified with Him, I am now able to live through Him.[10] Indeed, He is my very life.[11] He lives within me, and the life I now live I live by faith in your Son, Father. I love Him so much because I know He loves me, and He gave himself for me.[12]

As I pray in the name of Jesus, I know that you hear me, and I believe that nothing you desire shall be impossible to me.[13] I find all the treasures of wisdom and knowledge in your Son,[14] and He is everything to me. Thank you, Father, for giving all authority in heaven and in earth unto your Son, Jesus Christ, my Lord.[15] I realize it is that authority that becomes active when I pray in the name of Jesus.[16]

Almighty God, I praise you for highly exalting Jesus and giving Him a name which is above every name. It is at the name of Jesus, I realize, that every knee shall bow, and every tongue will confess that He is Lord to your glory, precious Father.[17] It is in His name, authority, power, and wisdom that I will always pray to you.

References: (1) John 15:16; (2) John 15:5; (3) Matthew 28:18; (4) Philippians 4:13; (5) Revelation 17:14; (6) John 14:6; (7) 1 Corinthians 1:30; (8) John 16:23-24; (9) John 3:16; (10) Galatians 2:20; (11) John 14:6; (12) Galatians 2:20; (13) Matthew 17:20; (14) Colossians 2:3; (15) Matthew 28:18; (16) John 15:7; (17) Philippians 2:9-10.

REMEMBER THIS: WHEN YOU PRAY IN THE NAME OF JESUS, NOTHING SHALL BE IMPOSSIBLE TO YOU. THIS IS BECAUSE NOTHING IS IMPOSSIBLE WITH GOD.

3

KEY # 3 – PRAY IN FAITH

But let him ask in faith, nothing wavering.
For he that wavereth is like a wave
of the sea driven with the wind and
tossed. For let not that man think
that he shall receive any thing
of the Lord. A double minded man
is unstable in all his ways.
(James 1:6-8)

Ask in Faith, Nothing Wavering

The fifteen prayer keys contained in this book are integral parts of an effective prayer life, but not one of them works without faith. The Bible says, "But without faith it is impossible to please Him, for he who comes to God must believe that He is, and that He is a rewarder of those who diligently seek Him" (Heb. 11:6, NKJV). The writer of Hebrews then goes on to give us a multitude of examples of faith in action, and what God accomplished through the faith of believers like Noah, Abel, Enoch, Abraham, Sarah, Jacob, Joseph, Moses, Rahab, Gideon, Barak, Samson, Jephthah, David, Samuel, and all the prophets. Some have accurately called this chapter in Hebrews: "Faith's Hall of Fame."

When we pray we must do so in profound faith, never wavering. Wavering, in this case, means doubting and losing heart. As we ask in faith, we see God in all His glory, as a Rewarder of all those who come to Him in faith. This is the foundation upon which all effective prayer is based: believing that God is, and that He is our Rewarder.

James wrote, "Every good gift and every perfect gift is from above, and comes down from the Father of lights, with whom there is no variation or shadow of turning" (James 1:17, NKJV). This is the assurance we have as believers: God is our Father. He never changes, and He wants to give us every good and perfect gift.

In fact, God has already given to us everything we need for godly living and praying. The Scriptures tell us, "Blessed be the God and Father of our Lord Jesus Christ, who has blessed us with every spiritual blessing in the heavenly places in Christ" (Eph. 1:3, NKJV). Notice that God *has already* blessed us with *every spiritual blessing* in the heavenly places in Christ! This is a powerful realization. Every spiritual blessing is already ours. Knowing this keeps us from wavering in our faith. Realizing this strengthens our faith because we know He has blessings already prepared for us!

The Essence of Faith

Faith, according to the dictionary, is belief in, trust in, and loyalty to God. It is also a firm belief that does not require scientific proof. Another definition tells us that faith is complete confidence in God. All of these dictionary meanings apply to our understanding of biblical faith as well. In fact, the Scriptures give us a vividly clear definition of faith: "Now faith is the substance of things hoped for, the evidence of things not seen" (Heb. 11:1).

Complete confidence in God. A firm belief. Trust in and loyalty to God. The substance of things hoped for, the evidence of things not seen. These six components of faith, when applied to our prayer life, bring amazing results. God always honors and rewards such strong faith.

After He had cursed the barren fig tree, Jesus admonished His disciples to have faith in God. He said, "Verily I say unto you, if ye have faith, and doubt not, ye shall not only do this which is done to the fig tree, but also if ye shall say unto this mountain, Be thou removed, and be thou cast into the sea; it shall be done" (Matt. 21:21). A faith-filled prayer is able to move mountains in our lives – figurative mountains in the form of seeming obstacles, difficulties, and dilemmas.

Praying in faith removes the mountains from our lives. These mountains represent anything standing in the way of God's perfect will being fulfilled in our lives. God gives us the faith to pray and He answers us by moving the mountains and showing us that He is able to do all things.

Faith Gives Us Access to God's Grace

Paul writes, "Therefore, having been justified by faith, we have peace with God through our Lord Jesus Christ, through whom also we have access by faith into this grace in which we stand, and rejoice in hope of the glory of God" (Rom. 5:1-2, NKJV).

This truth is reiterated in Ephesians 2:8-9: "For by grace you have been saved through faith, and that not of yourselves; it is the gift of God, not of works, lest anyone should boast" (NKJV). God's grace enables us to have faith, and to hold onto it even when times are difficult. His grace leads us to Him, and it keeps us in the center of His will.

Through faith we are able to inherit all the promises of God, as the Bible shows us: "That ye be not slothful, but followers of them who through faith and patience inherit the promises" (Heb. 6:12). One of those precious, God-given promises involves entering into

God's rest. The writer of the Book of Hebrews points out that it is faith that allows us to receive God's glorious promise of rest: "For we who have believed do enter that rest" (Heb. 4:3, NKJV). We cease from our own works, and enter into the blessed rest that comes through faith in God.

Disobedience, unbelief, and hardness of heart always prevent a person from entering the rest God has made available. It is only obtained through faith. Sometimes it is the inner restlessness we feel that leads us to God in the first place (and keeps on leading us to Him). Augustine prayed, "Our hearts are restless until they find their rest in thee, O God."

Concerning this rest, the writer of Hebrews goes on: "Let us therefore be diligent to enter that rest, lest anyone fall according to the same example of disobedience. For the word of God is living and powerful, and sharper than any two-edged sword, piercing even to the division of soul and spirit, and of joints and marrow, and is a discerner of the thoughts and intents of the heart" (Heb. 4:11-12, NKJV). The powerful Word of God opens the windows of faith for us. It shows us as we really are. It sheds light on the motives from which we operate, even in prayer.

In this same chapter of Hebrews we learn that Jesus Christ is our great High Priest,

". . .Who has passed through the heavens, Jesus the Son of God" (Heb. 4:14, NKJV). Because of this reality, we are able to hold fast to the confession of our faith, and we are motivated to respond to this marvelous invitation: "Let us therefore come boldly to the throne of grace, that we may obtain mercy and find grace to help in time of need" (Heb. 4:16, NKJV). Jesus, as our great High Priest, prays for us, and He shows us that our place of hope, consolation, and provision is God's throne of grace, the only place where we can find the help we need. This kind of confidence and boldness in prayer stem from faith in God and His Word.

Corrie ten Boom was a young lady when she and her sister, Betsy, and their father were rounded up by the Nazis and taken to the prison camp at Ravensbruck. It was a terrifying time for this Christian family from Holland. Corrie and the companion she was with were ordered to remove their clothing in preparation for a shower, which was to be followed with a thorough search of their clothing and bodies.

Corrie had her beloved Bible with her, and she knew that it would be taken from her if it were discovered, so she prayed in faith, asking God for wisdom and protection. After her shower, she tried to hide the Bible under her dress, but this resulted in an obvious bulge. Nonetheless, she felt perfect peace as she and her companion joined the line of women to be searched.

The guards completely removed the clothing from some of the women. The woman right in front of Corrie had hidden a woolen vest under her dress, and the guards took the vest and the dress, leaving the woman completely unclothed. Corrie whispered to her companion, "The Lord is busy answering our prayers. We won't have to surrender all our clothes." In her heart, Corrie knew that they would not find her precious Bible either.

She prayed again, "Lord, make your angels surround me. Make them solid today so the guards can't see me." God heard and answered her heart-felt cry. Corrie wrote, "But the guards let me pass, because they didn't even see me."

Again, as the two women left the building, Nazi guards conducted searches. They frisked the bodies of each woman who passed them. Corrie felt safe. She knew God would take care of the situation. Later, she wrote, "But I knew they would not see me for the angels were still surrounding me. I wasn't even surprised when I walked right by, unchecked. I stayed calm, but within me there rose a joyful prayer of thanks. 'O Lord, if this is the way you answer prayer, I can face even Ravensbruck without fear.'"

Faith Believes and Receives

In the gospels there are many instances of Jesus healing people. Each time faith was an integral part of the healing process. For example, a Canaanite woman sought Jesus' help for her demon-possessed daughter. In faith she cried out, "Lord, help me!" Jesus responded, "O woman, great is your faith! Let it be to you as you desire" (Matt. 15:28, NKJV). Jesus healed her daughter at that very moment. The mother's prayer was brief, but her faith was persistent, and Jesus rewarded her prayer of faith.

He said, "For assuredly, I say to you, whoever says to this mountain, 'Be removed and be cast into the sea,' and does not doubt in his heart, but believes that those things he says will be done, he will have whatever he says. Therefore I say to you, whatever things you ask when you pray, believe that you receive them, and you will have them" (Mark 11:23-24, NKJV).

Jesus says that we are to believe that we receive when we pray. Jesus knows more about prayer and faith than anyone. He told His disciples that He only spoke what the

Father taught Him. So, God is saying that believing prayer actually receives the answer by faith when we pray.

This concept is very challenging for us because many times we might prefer to have the answer first. The world says, "Seeing is believing," but Jesus says that we are to believe His Word regardless of what we see, and then we receive the answer we seek.

Yes, faith believes and faith *receives* and lets God do the rest!

**Be Strong in Faith,
Giving Glory to God**

The great patriarch of the Hebrew nation, Abraham, was a man of tremendous faith. He believed that God would guide him as he left Ur of the Chaldees in order to go to a land that God had promised to him. God made him "the father of many nations" because of his obedience and faith. Paul writes about Abraham's faith: "Therefore it is of faith that it might be according to grace, so that the promise might be sure to all the seed, not only to those who are of the law, but also to those who are of the faith of Abraham, who is the father of us all (as it is written, 'I have made you a father of many nations') in the presence of Him whom he believed—God, who gives life to the dead and calls those things which do not exist as though they did; who, contrary to hope, in hope believed, so that he became the father of many nations" (Rom. 4:16-18, NKJV).

God promised that He would bless the elderly Abraham and Sarah with a son, and Paul explains, "And not being weak in faith, he did not consider his own body, already dead (since he was about a hundred years old), and the deadness of Sarah's womb. He did not waver at the promise of God through unbelief, but was strengthened in faith, giving glory to God, and being fully convinced that what He had promised He was also able to perform" (Rom. 4:19-21, NKJV).

This is true faith, and it is faith in action. God gives life to the dead, and He calls those things which seem not to exist as though they do. In other words, from every practical, scientific point of view, it seemed impossible for the centenarian to conceive a child, but Bible faith knows no such limitations. With God all things are possible. (See Matt. 19:26.) God blessed the faith of Abraham, and He gave Sarah the promised blessing of a son.

Whatsoever Is Not of Faith Is Sin

Paul assures us, "So then faith cometh by hearing, and hearing by the word of God" (Rom. 10:17). It has been accurately stated that the more we get into the Word of God, the more God's faith gets into us. As we pore over the Scriptures, we meditate upon the multitude of God's promises, and our faith is strengthened, much as it was in Abraham's life, leading us to glorify God at every possible opportunity.

This is a process that cannot be analyzed by science, western rationalism, psychology, or psychiatry. It is completely spiritual and supernatural. The Bible says, ". . .for whatsoever is not of faith is sin" (Rom. 14:23). This, most certainly, includes our life of prayer which must be rooted and grounded in full faith and confidence in God's Word to us. Prayer without faith is like a kite without wind.

The importance of praying in faith is further explained to us in 1 Thessalonians 2:13: "For this cause also thank we God without ceasing, because, when ye received the word of God which ye heard of us, ye received it not as the word of men, but as it is in truth, the word of God, which effectually worketh also in you that believe." Unlike any other book, the Bible is the Word of God. Our responsibility to His Word is to read it, use it, claim it, choose it, believe it, live it, meditate upon it, memorize it, incorporate it into our prayer life, act upon it, stand upon its promises, preach it, teach it, and hide it in our hearts. As we do so, the Word of God will work effectively within us and within all the circumstances we face.

Many people see their life as consisting only of material and tangible things, and this certainly confines their perspective to the things of this earth, but the believer sees all of life from a different perspective than this, as the Bible states, "While we look not at the things which are seen, but at the things which are not seen: for the things which are seen are temporal; but the things which are not seen are eternal" (2 Cor. 4:18). The eyes of faith enable us to see those things which are eternal.

The Prayer of Faith

About prayer for wisdom James writes, "But let him ask in faith, nothing wavering. For he that wavereth is like a wave of the sea driven with the wind and tossed. For let not that man think that he shall receive any thing of the Lord" (James 1:6-7).

The prayer of faith never wavers. It remains focused and centered on the truths of God's Word. It boldly claims God's promises, knowing that they are the rightful inheritance of every child of God.

Faith, through the blood of Jesus, gives us both confidence and boldness. "Having therefore, brethren, boldness to enter into the holiest by the blood of Jesus, by a new and living way, which he hath consecrated for us, through the veil, that is to say, his flesh, and having an high priest over the house of God; let us draw near with a true heart in full assurance of faith, having our hearts sprinkled from an evil conscience, and our bodies washed with pure water. Let us hold fast the profession of our faith without wavering; (for he is faithful that promised)" (Heb. 10:19-23).

The confidence and boldness that come from faith reaches out to receive all that God has for us. In Jesus Christ, ". . .we have boldness and access with confidence by the faith of him" (Eph. 3:12).

This is the prayer of faith, energized by God's Word and propelled by faith in our Lord and Savior Jesus Christ. This prayer is one of full confidence in the Word of God and all its promises. It enables us to receive all the wonderful things God has for us. The prayer of faith is the person of faith's resource in times of need because he or she knows, "The effective, fervent prayer of a righteous man avails much" (James 5:16, NKJV).

Faith Is the Victory

Victorious living and praying result from strong faith. The Bible declares: "For whatsoever is born of God overcometh the world: and this is the victory that overcometh the world, even our faith" (1 John 5:4). This promise holds profound implications for our life of prayer. Through faith-filled praying we are able to overcome the world, even change the world, and we are able to experience victory over all foes. Praying in faith makes us overcomers in the world, victorious members of the family of God who know that their enemy is a defeated foe.

It is faith that permits us to wage an effective spiritual campaign against all the forces of the enemy, and every form of temptation and evil. The prayer of faith gives us:

God's provision, God's protection, God's power, God's comfort, God's authority, God's mercy, God's strength, God's wisdom, God's love, God's promises, God's presence, God's compassion, God's peace, God's rest, God's glory, God's forgiveness, God's grace, God's purity, God's mercy, God's providence, God's good and perfect gifts, God's healing, God's miracles, God's hope, God's ways, and God's life.

Charles H. Spurgeon wrote, "All the purposes of man have been defeated, but not the purposes of God. The promises of man may be broken – many of them are made to be broken – but the promises of God shall all be fulfilled. He is a promise-maker, but He never was a promise-breaker. He is a promise-keeping God, and every one of His people shall prove it to be so. This is my grateful, personal confidence, 'The Lord *will* fulfill his purpose for me.'. . . 'I, among the blood-wash'd throng, shall wave the palm, and wear the crown, and shout the loud victory.'"

Nothing Is Too Hard for God

The Prophet Jeremiah quotes our God as saying, "I am the Lord, the God of all flesh: is there anything too hard for me?" (Jer. 32:27). This is a rhetorical question – one that does not require an answer, except within the heart of each individual. How would the world be changed if every person literally believed that nothing is too hard for God?

The Psalmist declares, "God has spoken once, twice I have heard this: that power belongs to God" (Ps. 62:11, NKJV). All power and authority in heaven and earth belongs to God. He is the ever-able God who can do anything and everything. A person who prays believing this is a valiant prayer warrior in the Kingdom of God.

Our God is an awesome God. Remember as you pray that power belongs to Him, and all that He has is ours for the asking. Jesus said, "Ask, and it shall be given you" (Matt. 7:7).

Then He went on to unfold this truth further for us by giving us a glimpse into the Father's heart: "If ye then, being evil, know how to give good gifts unto your children, how much more shall your Father which is in heaven give good things to them that ask him?" (Matt. 7:11).

The key is faith, and faith is activated by simply asking. James affirms this when he writes, "Ye have not, because ye ask not" (James 4:2). The early disciples knew the vast importance of praying in faith. Indeed, they committed themselves to prayer: "We will give ourselves continually to prayer, and to the ministry of the word" (Acts 6:4).

The secret of their power to turn the world upside down is found in their great faith, and in their resolve to give themselves to prayer. "They continued steadfastly in prayers" (Acts 2:42).

Our all-powerful God tells us, "Ask and it shall be given to you." What an invitation this really is. As we put the key of faith into the door of His treasure house, we turn that key with prayer, and the door swings open wide. We walk through the door and we are able to receive those things that God has been storing up for us.

R.A. Torrey writes, "There is mighty power in prayer. It has much to do with our obtaining fullness of power in Christian life and service. Whoever will not take time for prayer may as well give up all hope of obtaining the fullness of power God has for him. . . .No matter what the time or the place, if we are to know fullness of power, we must be men and women of prayer."

Praying in faith, then, is praying in power. It is praying with the confidence and boldness that comes from a child-like trust in our heavenly Father. Praying in faith is praying in the certainty that God hears and answers our prayers.

As we continue to consider the keys to effective prayer, let us be sure to remember these extraordinarily outstanding words: "No eye has seen, no ear has heard, no mind has conceived what God has prepared for those who love him" (1 Cor. 2:9, NIV).

Charles H. Spurgeon developed a helpful analogy to give us insight into praying in faith. He wrote, "Faith goes up the stairs that love has made and looks out of the windows which hope has opened."

God has given us innumerable promises in His Word. He is faithful and trustworthy. Our responsibility is to respond to His ability through faith-filled prayer, and to do what He commands. Faith tells us, "God cannot fail.

Nothing is impossible with Him. He does all things well." Unless we actualize that faith in our hearts, however, God is not able to move.

Imagine the unlimited potential inherent in a prayer life that actualizes, appropriates, and acts upon all the promises of God's glorious Word. Such a prayer life is praying in faith, and it leads us to know that nothing is impossible with God, and nothing shall be impossible to us as well. (See Matt. 17:20.)

Prayer of Application

Almighty God, thank you for the example of Jesus who assures me, "According to your faith be it unto you."[1] Strengthen my faith as I give heed to your Word.[2] Your Word gives me great confidence, Father, and because of the faith it imparts to me I am certain that you hear me when I pray according to your Word.[3] Thank you, Lord God, for hearing and answering my prayers.

As my faith increases through your Word I pray for greater wisdom, Father. I ask for your wisdom in faith, nothing wavering, because I know that a wavering person cannot ever receive from you.[4] I come to you in faith, knowing that you are there, Father, and that you are a great Rewarder to me as I seek you in faith.[5]

When doubt tries to enter my mind, I will cast it away from me, Father, because I know that it is trying to exalt itself against you.[6] I choose to believe you and your Word, which is a lamp unto my feet and a light unto my path.[7] Help me to remember that the just shall live by faith, Father.[8]

It is my strong desire, Lord God, to continue in faith, grounded and settled, and to never be moved away from the hope of your gospel.[9] Give me all that I need to remain steadfast in my faith, Father, walking in Christ and rooted and built up in Him.[10] Establish me in the faith as I abound in thanksgiving for your great gifts to me.[11]

Father, thank you for revealing yourself to me in so many ways – through your Word,[12] your Spirit,[13] nature itself,[14] and all the miraculous changes you've wrought in my life. I believe in you with all my heart, and I purpose to continually walk in faith each day, for I know that it is faith which gives me the victory that overcomes the world.[15] How thankful I am that you have enabled me to be a believer, Father. With your help, I will walk in faith throughout my life.

References: (1) Matthew 9:29; (2) 1 Peter 5:10; (3) Romans 10:17; (4) James 1:5-8; (5) Hebrews 11:6; (6) 2 Corinthians 10:5; (7) Psalms 119:105; (8) Habakkuk 2:4; (9) Colossians 1:23; (10) Colossians 2:6-7; (11) James 1:17;

4
KEY # 4 – PERSISTENCE IN PRAYER

*Let us hold fast the profession of our faith
without wavering; (for he is faithful that
promised;). . . .Cast not away therefore your
confidence, which hath great recompence of
reward. For ye have need of patience, that, after
ye have done the will of God, ye might receive the
promise. For yet a little while, and he that shall
come will come, and will not tarry.*
(Heb. 10:23, 35-37)

Keeping On Keeping On

An anonymous writer describes persistence in prayer as follows: "How glibly we talk of praying without ceasing! Yet, we are quite ready to quit if our prayer remains unanswered but a week or a month! We assume that by a stroke of His arm or an action of His will, God will give us what we ask. It never seems to dawn on us that He is the Master of nature, as of grace, and that, sometimes He chooses one way, and sometimes another, to do His work. It takes years, sometimes, to answer a prayer. When it is answered, we can look back to see that it did take years. But God knows all the time. It is His will that we pray, and pray, and still pray, and so come to know indeed what it is to pray without ceasing."

This is what persistence is all about – the quality of keeping on keeping on, to go on resolutely even in the face of opposition. Persistence also involves remaining unchanged or fixed with regard to the subjects we are praying about. Persistence is strengthened by our confidence that our prayers will be heard and answered when we know that we are praying in faith according to the will of God, and in the name of Jesus.

The element of patience is an implicit part of persistence in prayer. We must be willing to wait for God's perfect timing in response to our prayers. We must be willing to persevere in faith. God rewards this kind of persistence as the story of the importunate widow points out: "There was in a certain city a judge who did not fear God nor regard man. Now there was a widow in that city; and she came to him, saying, 'Get justice for me from my adversary.' And he would not for a while; but afterward he said within himself, 'Though I do not fear God nor regard man, yet because this widow troubles me I will avenge her, lest by her continual coming she weary me'" (Luke 18:2-5, NKJV).

This widow was persistent, and the ungodly judge, wearied by her continual pleas, decided to avenge her. This man had no regard for God or man, but he did understand persistence. If he, being evil, would respond in this way, how much more will our heavenly Father gladly respond to our persistence in prayer? God loves for us to be persistent. This kind of persistence is based on our believing that God loves us and wants to help us.

Jesus said, "Ask, and it will be given to you; see, and you will find, knock, and it will be opened to you. For everyone who asks receives, and he who seeks finds, and to him who knocks it will be opened. Or what man is there among you who, if his son asks for bread, will give him a stone? Or if he asks for a fish, will he give him a serpent? If you then, being evil, know how to give good gifts to your children, how much more will your Father who is in heaven give good things to those who ask him!" (Matt. 7:7-11, NKJV).

One of the finest scriptural examples of persistence in prayer is given to us by Jacob in the Book of Genesis: "And Jacob was left alone; and there wrestled a man with him until the breaking of the day. And when he saw that he prevailed not against him, he touched the hollow of his thigh; and the hollow of Jacob's thigh was out of joint, as he wrestled with him. And he said, Let me go, for the day breaketh. And he said, I will not let thee go, except thou bless me" (Gen. 32:24-26). This is persistence combined with unswerving resolve, and when we apply it to prayer, it enables us to prevail as Jacob did when he wrestled with this man who may have been an angel of God.

We are encouraged to seek the Lord and His strength, ". . .to seek His face continually" (1 Chron. 16:11). Such resolve in seeking God's face is an integral part of prevailing prayer. It is true that persistent, believing prayer prevails.

The Bible is full of examples of persistence in prayer. Moses prayed forty days and nights in his earnest efforts to stay God's hand against the disobedience of the Israelites. Abraham interceded repeatedly for the salvation of Sodom and Gomorrah. Elijah repeated his prayer seven times before rain clouds appeared. Daniel prayed for three weeks before his answer and blessing came. Such persistence does bring results, as the following contemporary example points out.

The doctors had told our friend Nancy that she would never have children. She and her husband, Bob, began to pray. They believed that God would give them children, and they felt that He would do so in His way, according to His time schedule. They trusted God to help them.

Every day they would join their hands together and ask God to bless them with a child. They did this for more than four years. Other people would say, "Nancy, maybe God wants you to adopt a child. Perhaps that's His will for you." Though neither Nancy nor Bob had a problem with the thought of adopting a child, they both felt that God would enable Nancy to become pregnant.

God heard their persistent, faith-filled prayers, and one morning Nancy went to the gynecologist's offce for her regular appointment. He said, "Let's do a pregnancy test." The test was positive, and Nancy and Bob rejoiced in the faithfulness of God. Their physician remarked, "This truly is a miracle."

The believing couple had a baby boy, and they named him Robert, Jr. Two years later, they adopted a little girl. Bob and Nancy know the power of persistent prayer, and they are filled with gratitude to their heavenly Father who gave them the desires of their heart.

Pray Without Ceasing

As believers, we are admonished to: "Rejoice always, pray without ceasing, in everything give thanks; for this is the will of God in Christ Jesus for you" (1 Thess. 5:16-18, NKJV). It is clearly God's will for us to pray without ceasing. This means that we should live in an attitude of prayer at all times. Prayer then becomes as natural as breathing to us; it is continual, it is active, and it is a natural response to the circumstances of life.

Therefore, "Praying *always* with all prayer and supplication in the Spirit, being watchful to this end with all perseverance and supplication for all the saints. . ." (Eph. 6:18, NKJV), we live out the life of prayer minute by minute and day by day. It is as Edward Payson wrote, "Prayer is the first thing, the second thing, the third thing necessary. . . .Pray, then, my dear brother, pray, pray, pray."

Paul wrote, "Continue in prayer, and watch in the same with thanksgiving" (Col. 4:2). The word "watch," as Paul uses it here, involves the kind of patience that is a fruit of the Spirit in our lives: "But the fruit of the Spirit is love, joy, peace, longsuffering [patience], kindness, goodness, faithfulness, gentleness, self-control" (Gal. 5:22-23, NKJV).

Patience in Prayer

Persistence in prayer and patience in prayer are vitally linked to each other. The Psalmist tells us to "Wait on the Lord" (Ps. 27:14). Daniel shows us what happens when we wait on the Lord: "Blessed is he that waiteth" (Dan. 12:12). Habakkuk gives us a divine assurance about patience in prayer when he writes, "Though it tarry, wait for it; because it will surely come" (Hab. 2:3).

Charles Finney wrote, "You must persevere. You are not to pray for a thing once and then cease, and call that the prayer of faith." In a similar vein, through Zephaniah, God said, "Wait ye upon Me, saith the Lord, until the day that I rise up to the prey" (Zeph. 3:8).

There is a place in prayer where you pray until you know in your heart that God has undertaken on your behalf. This is the time when you know inside that it's as good as done. Then you go from petitions to praise, thanking God for His goodness and His faithfulness.

It is clear that patience and persistence go hand in hand. Jesus commanded His disciples, "Wait for the promise of the Father" (Acts 1:4). Through persistence and patience in prayer we learn many things about God, and our relationship with Him becomes much more intimate and fruitful, partly because our focus is not simply on receiving as much as it is on believing and loving Him.

We want to remember that it isn't always the goal that is the most important thing to God; sometimes it's the journey on the way to the goal. That is where character is developed, where relationship blossoms, where faith is deepened down to the very core of our being.

Paul wrote, "Tribulation worketh patience; and patience, experience; and experience, hope" (Rom. 5:3-4). Patiently persisting in prayer leads us to a deeper hope in God. We need patience, as the writer of Hebrews points out, "Ye have need of patience, that, after ye have done the will of God, ye might receive the promise" (Heb. 10:36). This is a wonderful assurance from the Word of God. We will receive God's promises when we exercise patient persistence in prayer.

We are able to have patience in prayer when we realize how faithful the Father is to His children. Through patient prayer we are able to cultivate the attitude of David who prayed, "Thou hast dealt well with thy servant, O Lord, according unto thy word" (Ps. 119:65).

When Kathleen was facing a very serious battle related to her health, she prayed over and over again for several months, "God, I know you are faithful. I know you love me, and I believe you are healing me."

God heard her prayers, and He honored her persistence by giving her complete healing and increased faith. Many times the enemy would try to undermine her faith by suggesting that healing was not going to happen, but Kathleen kept holding on to God's hand and believing His Word was true.

As we pray, we must let our faith act upon these words: "Faithful is he that calleth you, who also will do it" (1 Thess. 5:24). God is awake at all times; He hears our prayers, and "He will not suffer thy foot to be moved: he that keepeth thee will not slumber. Behold, he that keepeth Israel shall neither slumber nor sleep" (Ps. 121:3-4).

Run With Endurance

In Hebrews we read, "Therefore we also, since we are surrounded by so great a cloud of witnesses, let us lay aside every weight, and the sin which so easily ensnares us, and let us run with endurance the race that is set before us, looking unto Jesus, the author and finisher of our faith, who for the joy that was set before Him endured the cross, despising the shame, and has sat down at the right hand of the throne of God" (Heb. 12:1-2, NKJV).

Endurance is an inner quality that is built into us as a result of persistence and patience. It entails continuing on and remaining firm in the face of all obstacles. The Bible promises us, "Therefore, my beloved brethren, be steadfast, immovable, always abounding in the work of the Lord, knowing that your labor is not in vain in the Lord" (1 Cor. 15:58, NKJV). Endurance is being steadfast and immovable as we abound in God's work, including prayer.

Peter encourages us to be diligent and persistent: "Therefore, beloved, looking forward to these things, be diligent to be found by Him in peace, without spot and blameless" (2 Pet. 3:14, NKJV). The implication is that persistence, patience, diligence, and perseverance lead to peace. This is personal peace that comes from knowing that God has everything under control, and because He does we can remain steadfast and enduring in prayer.

Richard Newton wrote, "Prayer and patience and faith are never disappointed. I have long since learned that if ever I was to be a minister, faith and prayer must make me one. When I can find my heart dissolved in prayer, everything else is relatively easy." This attitude of persistence and patience in prayer is never a disappointing experience for the child of God.

Prayer of Application

Almighty God, my heavenly Father, I come to you now with a heart filled with desire to seek your face continually,[1] to pray without ceasing,[2] and to rejoice evermore.[3] Thank you for making this possible for me.

I recognize my need for patience, Lord God, and so I ask you to help me not to be hasty in my spirit with regard to anything.[4] Let me be good ground for your Word, Father, so that with a good and honest heart I will hear your Word and keep it, because I know this will bring forth the fruit of patience in my life.[5] With a persistent attitude in prayer, I will strive to let patience have its perfect work in my life so that I will become complete and have no want for anything.[6]

O God, strengthen my hands.[7] I thank you that nothing shall ever be able to separate me from your love which I fully experience in Christ Jesus, my Lord.[8] With a firmness of my resolve, I purpose not to grow weary in well doing (including prayer), because I know you will make it possible for me to reap a good harvest in due time.[9] Thank you, Father.

Empower me to endure hardness as a good soldier of Jesus Christ.[10] I will hold fast the profession of my faith without wavering,[11] and I will run with patience the race that you have set before me.[12] Father, though your grace I will hope until the end.[13] Thank you for your promise that I will inherit all things, for you are my God and I am your child.[14]

References: (1) Deuteronomy 4:29; (2) 1 Thessalonians 5:17; (3) 1 Thessalonians 5:16; (4) Ecclesiastes 7:8-9; (5) Luke 8:15; (6) James 1:4; (7) Nehemiah 6:9; (8) Romans 8:38-39; (9) Galatians 6:9; (10) 2 Timothy 2:3; (11) Hebrews 10:23; (12) Hebrews 12:1; (13) 1 Peter 1:13; (14) Revelation 21:7.

5

KEY # 5 – BEING SPECIFIC IN PRAYER

*Have faith in God. For assuredly, I say
to you, whoever says to this mountain,
'Be removed and be cast into the sea,'
and does not doubt in his heart, but
believes that those things he says will
be done, he will have whatever he says.
Therefore I say to you, whatever things
you ask when you pray, believe that
you receive them, and you will have them.*
(Mark 11:22-24, NKJV)

Specific Faith for Specific Things

A vague, general prayer is never as effective as a specific and definite prayer. E.M. Bounds wrote, "Faith and prayer select the subjects to be prayed for thus determining what God is to do. 'He shall have whatsoever he saith.' Christ is ready to supply exactly and fully all the demands of faith and of prayer. If the order to God is clear, specific, and definite, God will fit it exactly in agreement with the terms put before Him."

This is an interesting concept, isn't it? Someone might ask, "Does prayer really work this way?" The answer is yes, when it is the prayer of faith prayed from a heart surrendered to God and His will. As we feed on God's Word He imparts faith to our hearts. Hebrews 4:12 says that the Word separates soulish thoughts from spiritual thoughts. In this way the Word brings clarity to our hearts and minds and helps us to discern God's will in a matter. Then we begin to develop a faith-sensitivity concerning the things that we can pray for and receive with integrity of heart.

The faith-sensitivity thus acquired helps us also to know when we should pray for certain things. The Word gives us faith from God, and the Holy Spirit reveals the timing of God to us. We always want the Holy Spirit to be our Guide in prayer.

It is, however, possible to pray wrongly and not receive. James tells us, "You ask and do not receive, because you ask amiss, that you may spend it on your pleasures" (See James 4:3, NKJV). What are we to do if we pray amiss? Repent, and ask God for clarity on the matter. He is always ready to help us if we will be humble and teachable. He always gives His grace to the humble. (See James 4:6.) Therefore, Love God with all your heart and be specific when you pray.

Paul wrote about this as well: "Be careful [anxious] for nothing; but in every thing by prayer and supplication with thanksgiving let your requests be made known unto God" (Phil. 4:6). Specific requests for specific things. The result of such specificity in prayer will be: "And the peace of God, which passeth all understanding, shall keep your hearts and minds through Christ Jesus" (Phil. 4:7).

Specific Promises – Specific Prayers

God's great and precious promises are always specific and definite. They do not need interpretation, because they are simple and direct statements from the Father's heart to His children. As we focus on His promises we are empowered to pray in accord with their specific truths.

E.M. Bounds writes, "Prayer and the promises are interdependent. The promise inspires and energizes prayer, but prayer locates the promise, and gives it realization and location. The promise is like the blessed rain falling in full showers, but prayer, like the pipes, which transmit, preserve and direct the rain, localizes and precipitates these promises, until they become local and personal, and bless, refresh and fertilize. Prayer takes hold of the promise and conducts it to its marvelous ends, removes the obstacles, and makes a highway for the promise to its glorious fulfillment.

"While God's promises are 'exceeding great and precious,' they are specific, clear and personal."

Let's take a look at some of God's promises regarding prayer. Notice how each one is very specific, and God intends for each of us to apply the promise to our own personal prayer life.

"Ask, and it shall be given you; seek, and ye shall find; knock, and it shall be opened unto you" (Luke 11:9).

"But thou, when thou prayest, enter into thy closet, and when thou hast shut thy door, pray to the Father which is in secret; and thy Father which seeth in secret shall reward thee openly" (Matt. 6:6).

"For the eyes of the Lord are over the righteous, and his ears are open unto their prayers" (1 Pet. 3:12).

"And this is the confidence that we have in him, that, if we ask any thing according to his will, he heareth us: And if we know that he hear us, whatsoever we ask, we know that we have the petitions that we desired of him" (1 John 5:14-15).

"My voice shalt thou hear in the morning, O Lord; in the morning will I direct my prayer unto thee, and will look up" (Ps. 5:3).

"But know that the Lord hath set apart him that is godly for himself: the Lord will hear when I call unto him" (Ps. 4:3).

"Give ear, O Lord, unto my prayer; and attend to the voice of my supplications. In the day of my trouble I will call upon thee: for thou wilt answer me" (Ps. 86:6-7).

"So shall my word be that goeth forth out of my mouth: it shall not return unto me void, but it shall accomplish that which I please, and it shall prosper in the thing whereto I sent it" (Isa. 55:11).

"Cast thy bread upon the waters: for thou shalt find it after many days" (Eccles. 11:1).

"And I will give thee the treasures of darkness, and hidden riches of secret places, that thou mayest know that I, the Lord, which call thee by thy name, am the God of Israel" (Isa. 45:3).

"Call unto me, and I will answer thee, and shew thee great and mighty things, which thou knowest not" (Jer. 33:3).

The preceding verses are marvelous prayer promises from the Word of God. They tell us that God will respond to our asking, seeking, and knocking. He will reward us openly. His ears are open to our prayers. He will grant our petitions. He will answer our prayers. His Word will accomplish its purposes in our lives, and it will prosper by never returning to Him void. God will give us the treasures of darkness and the hidden riches of secret places. He will show us mighty things that we have never known.

These are but a few of the prayer promises in the Bible, and as we incorporate these (as well as all the other promises regarding specific things that God will do for us) into our prayer life, God will respond by giving us what we are asking for.

A pastor friend of ours named John started his ministry in a very small church in the mountains of Virginia. The congregation was somewhat poor, and John's salary was quite small. The Volkswagen bus he was driving broke down, and he did not have enough money to have it repaired.

John began to pray. He later told us that his prayer went something like this: "Heavenly Father, I know you know all my needs. I need a new car. Today I saw an Oldsmobile at the dealer's which is being sold for $15,899.00. Dear God, you know I need that amount of money to buy this car. I believe you want me to have this car. I trust you to meet this need. In Jesus' name I pray, Amen."

This was a specific prayer for a specific need, and it required a specific amount of money. That afternoon a man from a nearby city knocked on the door of John's study. He introduced himself to the young pastor, and said, "I was driving along the interstate and I saw the steeple of your church. I felt that God was telling me to pull off, because there was someone there who needed my help."

This man was a member of a Christian businessman's organization, and he had felt led to make a financial contribution to the pastor. He took out his checkbook and then asked, "Pastor, what is your need?"

A bit hesitantly, the pastor said, "Well, I was just praying for a new car, because my vehicle seems to be beyond repair. The car I would like to purchase costs $15,899.00. I know that's a lot of money, but I believe God wants to meet this need."

"That's why He sent me to you," the businessman happily responded. He then sat down and wrote out a check in the amount of $16,000.00. "Pastor, you go ahead and buy that car, and while you're at it, get yourself some lunch."

John cried as he embraced this new friend. From that time forth the businessman sent regular checks to the pastor. God does honor specific prayers that are based on our specific needs.

Our Awesome, Prayer-Answering God

The Bible is filled with examples of God's people praying for specific things. Likewise, the Bible is filled with God's specific answers to specific prayer requests. Some of those prayers and answers are cited below:

Abraham was specific in his prayer for a child. God gave him Isaac. (See Gen. 15-21.)

Jacob specifically asked God for deliverance from his brother Esau whom he feared. God did so, and He promised to make the seed of Jacob innumerable. (See Gen. 32.)

Rachel prayed for a child, and God answered by giving Joseph to her and Jacob. (See Gen. 30.)

Moses prayed that his enemies would be scattered, and God answered by sending fire to the camp of his enemies. Then Moses asked God to put out the fire, and He did so. (See Num. 11.)

Joshua asked God to make the sun stand still, and the Father did so. (See Josh. 10.)

Samson called out to God for strength, and the Lord God blessed him with supernatural power. (See Judg. 16.)

Manoah, like Abraham and Rachel before him, prayed for a child. God blessed him with Samson. (See Judg. 13.)

Similarly, Hannah asked for a man-child. Samuel was the answer to her prayer. (See 1 Sam. 1.)

Elijah asked God to send fire. The fire fell from heaven and consumed the burnt sacrifice, causing the people to know the reality of God's power. (See 1 Kings 18.)

Elisha asked God to bring the Shunammite's dead son back to life. God did so. (See 2 Kings 4.)

Jabez asked God to bless him by enlarging his coast. He prayed that God's hand would be with him and that He would keep him from evil. The answer: "And God granted him that which he requested" (1 Chron. 4:10).

King Jeroboam besought the Lord for healing. God heard his prayer and healed him. (See 1 Kings 13.)

Similarly, Hezekiah asked God to heal him. God granted his request. (See 2 Kings 20.)

Daniel asked God for revelation. God talked with him and gave him understanding. (See Dan. 9.)

Similarly, two blind men asked Jesus to have mercy upon them. He responded by touching their eyes and healing them. (See Matt. 9.)

Peter, who had been walking on the water, asked Jesus to save him when he began to sink. Jesus helped him, and rebuked his lack of faith. (See Matt. 14.)

The centurion asked Jesus to heal his servant. The Lord did so, and then he complimented the centurion's faith. (See Luke 7.)

A nobleman asked Jesus to heal his son. The Master responded with compassion and total healing. (See John 4.)

Jesus prayed, calling Lazarus to come forth from the tomb. God answered, and raised Lazarus from the dead. (See John 11.)

A common thief who was crucified alongside Jesus asked the Lord to remember him in heaven. Jesus promised the criminal that he would join Him in paradise. (See Luke 23.)

Believers asked God to get Peter released from prison. God sent an angel to deliver him. (See Acts 12.)

Paul prayed for Publius' father. God heard his prayer, and the man was healed. Others were healed as well. (See Acts 28.)

Paul and Silas sang praises to God in their prison cell. The Lord God sent an earthquake which enabled them to go free. (See Acts 16.)

The preceding are but a few examples of answered prayer in the Bible. There are many more. Notice two things about each of these cases: the prayers were specific and they were full of faith. In each case God granted the pray-er's specific requests, and he will do the same for us.

In response to specific prayers, barren women gave birth, enemies were defeated, deliverance was granted, the sun stood still, fire fell from heaven, the dead were raised, multitudes were healed, revelation and spiritual understanding were imparted, eternal life was imparted, believers were released from prison, God sent earthquakes, and the faith of many was strengthened.

Truly, our God is an awesome God!

Prayer of Application

Heavenly Father, help me to remember the importance of keeping my prayer requests specific and direct. With this in mind, I now pray specifically for the following:_____

_____

_____

_____. Thank you for hearing[1] and answering my prayer.[2]

As I incline my ear to the words of your Word I will not let them depart from my eyes, and I will keep them within my heart, because I know your Word is life and health unto me.[3]

As I learn to pray with greater specificity, Father, I ask you to bring to my remembrance the specific truths of your Word so that I will pray your powerful Word and claim your specific promises.[4] I thank you that you always answer your promises with a resounding yes and amen.[5]

Your Word is the joy and rejoicing of my heart. Thank you for calling me by your name, O Lord God of hosts.[6] Help me to abide in Jesus and to let your Word abide in me, because I know that this is a great key to answered prayer, and you have promised that you will grant my requests if I do so.[7]

Father, I have great confidence that you will grant my petitions as I learn to pray according to your Word and your will.[8] Thank you for hearing my prayers.[9] The answered prayers within your Word show me how powerful and awesome you are, mighty Father.[10] As you guide me, Lord God, I will pray for the specific things that you promise to me, and I know you will grant my requests.[11]

References: (1) 1 Kings 8:30; (2) 2 Kings 20:5; (3) Proverbs 4:20-23; (4) John 14:26; (5) 2 Corinthians 1:20; (6) Jeremiah 15:16; (7) John 15:7; (8) 1 John 5:14; (9) Hebrews 4:16; (10) Hebrews 4:12; (11) 1 John 5:14-15.

REMEMBER THIS: WHEN YOU BRING SPECIFIC REQUESTS TO THE FATHER, HIS SPECIFIC PROMISES FOR YOU ARE ACTIVATED IN YOUR BEHALF.

KEY # 6 – PRAYING IN
THE SPIRIT

*Praying always with all prayer and
supplication in the Spirit, and
watching thereunto with all
perseverance for all saints.*
(Eph. 6:18)

Praying Always

The above verse reiterates the importance
of continuity in prayer as we have already
discussed in chapter 4, which deals with
persistence in prayer. The Bible tells us to pray
incessantly, and this is echoed by Paul when
he says, "Praying *always* with all prayer and
supplication. . ." (Eph. 6:18). Praying *always* is
an important part of praying in the Spirit.

Again, we see the idea of persistence and
perseverance being an important part of
praying in the Spirit. We pray in the Spirit and
we persevere until we see what we are
praying for come to fruition in our life and the
lives of others.

Supplication in the Spirit

A supplicant is one who makes a humble
entreaty before one who is in authority. The

formal request he or she makes is known as a supplication. Humility and earnestness are integral parts of such a prayer. When we make a supplication before our heavenly Father we must do so earnestly, in a spirit of persistence, confidence, and humility.

An earnest pray-er is one who is guided by a sense of intensity, seriousness, and zeal. Such a person is intent on seeing his or her prayers answered, and approaches prayer with a deep sense of its importance in his or her life.

Such earnestness, intensity, seriousness of purpose, persistence, humility, and confidence are characteristics of praying in the Spirit.

Watching in Prayer

The verb *watching* implies active vigilance on the part of the believer. Praying in the Spirit, therefore, is watching and waiting for God's answer to come forth, as it surely will.

G. H. Morgan wrote, "During the great Welsh Revival a minister was said to be very successful in winning souls by one sermon that he preached – hundreds were converted. Far away in a valley news reached a brother minister of the marvelous success of this sermon. He desired to find out the secret of the man's great success – He walked the long way, and came to the minister's poor cottage, and the first thing he said was, 'Brother, where did you get that sermon?' He was taken into a poorly furnished room and pointed to a spot where the carpet was worn threadbare, near a window that looked out upon the everlasting hills and solemn mountains and said, 'Brother, there is where I got that sermon. My heart was heavy for men. One night I knelt there – and cried for power as I never prayed before. The hours passed until midnight struck, and the stars looked down on a sleeping world, but the answer came not. I prayed on until I saw a faint streak of grey shoot up, then it was silver – silver became purple and gold. Then the sermon came and the power came and men fell under the influence of the Holy Spirit."

Notice the watchfulness (all night long), and the persistent, incessant praying of the minister. The result was the power of the Holy Spirit, and his next sermon was so anointed that hundreds of men fell under that same power. This is praying in the Spirit – prayers of zeal, watchfulness, persistence, and power.

In this kind of prayer we begin by obeying God's command to pray. We know He wants to meet us there. We give ourselves to the task, and look to the Holy Spirit within to produce the prayers that He desires. We yield ourselves to the Spirit's flow within us.

We read, "But you shall receive power when the Holy Spirit has come upon you. . ." (Acts 1:8). This is spiritual power for witnessing, preaching, living, and praying. It is so intense and dynamic that it results in full and lasting change in our lives and in the lives of those for whom we are praying.

The Holy Spirit, Our Teacher

Jesus prayed, asking the Father to send His Comforter (the Holy Spirit) to us so that we would be endued with power from on high, would experience His comforting presence, would be able to witness effectively, and be reminded of all that Jesus has taught us.

These are some aspects of the Holy Spirit's work in our lives. To receive the fullness of the Holy Spirit we must pray. To be led by the Holy Spirit we must pray. To be used by the Holy Spirit we must pray. To be anointed by the Holy Spirit we must pray. The Holy Spirit and prayer are inextricably linked with each other.

The Holy Spirit is our Teacher in everything, especially prayer. Jude writes, "But ye, beloved, building up yourselves on your most holy faith, praying in the Holy Ghost, keep yourselves in the love of God, looking for the mercy of our Lord Jesus Christ unto eternal life" (Jude 1:20-21).

Jesus makes this concept clear for us: "Howbeit when he, the Spirit of truth, is come, he will guide you into all truth: for he shall not speak of himself; but whatsoever he shall hear, that shall he speak: and he will shew you things to come" (John 16:13). God, the Holy Spirit, will guide us into all truth by sharing the Father's heart with us. He will also give us glimpses into the future which will enable us to pray more effectively.

Likewise, the Holy Spirit is our Teacher regarding prayer. The great Apostle Paul puts it this way: "Likewise the Spirit also helpeth our infirmities: for we know not what we should pray for as we ought: but the Spirit itself maketh intercession for us with groanings which cannot be uttered. And he that searcheth the hearts knoweth what is the mind of the Spirit, because he maketh intercession for the saints according to the will of God" (Rom. 8:26-27).

We have learned that Jesus is making intercession for us, and so is the Spirit of God. The Holy Spirit searches our hearts and makes intercession for us according to the will of God. This is a powerful promise, because we've already seen how important it is for our prayers to line up with God's will. The Holy Spirit helps us to keep our prayers on target, in line with our Father's will for us.

Archbishop Trench put it this way: "We must pray in the Spirit, in the Holy Ghost, if we would pray at all. Lay this, I beseech you, to heart. Do not address yourselves to prayer as to a work to be accomplished in your own natural strength. It is a work of God, of God the Holy Ghost, a work of His in you and by you, and in which you must be fellow-workers with Him – but His work notwithstanding."

Prayer empowered by the Holy Spirit becomes a true work of God, a masterpiece, if you will, in which the Holy Spirit and our spirits are united. Therefore, praying in the spirit (our spirit) is closely related to praying in the Spirit (the Holy Spirit).

E. M. Bounds writes, "The Holy Spirit helps us in our weaknesses, gives wisdom to our ignorance, turns ignorance into wisdom, and changes our weakness into strength. The Spirit Himself does this. He helps and takes hold with us as we tug and toil. He adds His wisdom to our ignorance, gives His strength to our weakness. He pleads for us and in us. He quickens, illumines and inspires our prayers. He indites and elevates the matter of our prayers, and inspires the words and feelings of our prayers. He works mightily in us so that we can pray mightily. He enables us to pray always and ever according to the will of God."

The Spirit of Revelation

The Holy Spirit is the Spirit of Revelation, and this fact relates directly to our life of prayer. Paul wrote, "But as it is written: 'Eye has not seen, nor ear heard, nor have entered into the heart of man the things which God has prepared for those who love Him.' But God has revealed them to us through His Spirit. For the Spirit searches all things, yes, the deep things of God. For what man knows the things of a man except the spirit of the man which is in him? Even so no one knows the things of God except the Spirit of God" (1 Cor. 2:9-11, NKJV). The Holy Spirit knows the things of God, and as He leads us in prayer, He reveals the heart of God to us. It is then that we begin to experience the things which God has prepared for those who love Him.

When our spirits are filled with the Spirit of God a new boldness comes to us in prayer. We understand what God wants; we get much closer to His will. This spiritual enlightenment and revelation enables us to pray with authority and strength. We are transported from praying according to our own will and desires into that wonderful realm of knowing what God's will is. This is praying in the Spirit.

E. M. Bounds shows us how this works: "We always pray according to the will of God when the Holy Spirit helps our praying. He prays through us only 'according to the will of God.' If our prayers are not according to the will of God they die in the presence of the Holy Spirit. He gives such prayers no countenance, no help. Discountenanced and unhelped by Him, prayers, not according to God's will, soon die out of every heart where the Holy Spirit dwells."

The Spirit of Supplication

The Holy Spirit is our life. His breath fills us with the life and power of God. To pray in the Spirit, therefore, is to pray in Spirit-inspired power. It is life-changing and life-producing prayer.

In *The Ministry of Intercession*, Andrew Murray writes, "'I will pour out the Spirit of supplication.' Are you beginning to see that the mystery of prayer is the mystery of the Divine indwelling? God in heaven gives His Spirit to be the Divine power praying in our hearts, drawing us upward to our God. God is a Spirit, and nothing but a similar life and Spirit within us can have communion with Him. Man was created for this communion with God, so that God could dwell and work in him, and be the life of his life. It was the Divine indwelling that sin lost. Christ came to exhibit it in His life, to win it back for us in His death, and then impart it to us by coming again from heaven in the Spirit to live in His disciples. Only this indwelling of God through the Spirit can explain and enable us to appropriate the wonderful promises given to prayer. God gives the Spirit as a Spirit of supplication, too, to maintain His Divine life within us as a life in which prayer continually rises to heaven."

Prayer of Application

Almighty God, my heavenly Father, I love you, and I know you love me.[1] Thank you so much for your love, and thank you for sending the Holy Spirit to be my Comforter[2] and Teacher.[3] I receive His help as I pray.

Fill me with your Holy Spirit, Father,[4] so that I will be able to pray more effectively and with power.[5] I want always to walk in the Holy Spirit for the rest of my days. Lord God, where He leads me, I will follow.[6]

It is my heart-felt desire, O God, to be led by your Spirit in prayer and in all aspects of my life.[7] Thank you for granting me that privilege, Father, and for giving me the Spirit of adoption whereby I am able to cry out, "Abba, Father,"[8] in the wonderful realization that you are my heavenly Father who cares about every aspect of my life.

Father, thank you for the indwelling of your Holy Spirit in my life which transforms me into your temple.[9] Thank you, Father, for this honor. May I never misrepresent your gospel or defile your temple in any way. I never want to bring dishonor to you, O God.

Thank you for the precious fruit of your Spirit in my life.[10] May others taste of your fruit, and hunger after you as I live and pray. The fruit of your Spirit in my life leads me into all goodness and righteousness and truth as I pray.[11]

As your Holy Spirit leads me, I will pray according to your will, and I know you will hear me and grant my supplications.[12] Thank you, God, for the power of the Holy Spirit in my life.

References: *(1) 1 John 4:19; (2) John 16:7; (3) John 14:26; (4) Ephesians 5:18; (5) Acts 1:8; (6) Luke 9:57-62; (7) Romans 8:15; (8) Galatians 4:6; (9) 1 Corinthians 3:16; (10) Galatians 5:22-25; (11) Ephesians 5:9; (12) 1 John 5:14-15.*

***REMEMBER THIS*: PRAYING IN THE SPIRIT, WITH ALL KINDS OF PRAYER AND SUPPLICATION, IS PRAYING IN SUPERNATURAL POWER THAT ALWAYS BRINGS RESULTS.**

7

KEY # 7 – WAITING ON GOD

But they that wait upon the Lord
shall renew their strength; they shall mount
up with wings as eagles; they shall run,
and not be weary; and they shall
walk, and not faint.
(Isa. 40:31)

Wait Only Upon God

The Psalmist wrote, "My soul, wait thou only upon God" (Ps. 62:1). Implicit in this good counsel are the following aspects: standing still, being quiet, exercising patience, persevering, being vigilant, standing fast, and believing. Andrew Murray helps us to see what waiting on God entails: "'Take heed, and be quiet: fear not, neither be faint-hearted.' 'In quietness and in confidence shall be your strength.' Such words reveal to us the close connection between quietness and faith. They show us what a deep need there is of quietness, the element of true waiting upon God. If we are to have our whole heart turned toward God, we must have it turned away from man, from all that occupies and interests, whether of joy or sorrow." (From *Waiting on God* by Andrew Murray.)

The Bible abounds with wonderful promises about waiting on God:

You will never be ashamed when you wait on God. "Thou shalt know that I am the Lord: for they shall not be ashamed that wait for me" (Isa. 49:23).

Waiting on God brings blessings into your life. "Blessed are all they that wait for him" (Isa. 30:18).

God will strengthen your heart. "Wait on the Lord: be of good courage, and he shall strengthen thine heart: wait, I say, on the Lord" (Ps. 27:14).

God will be your help and your shield when you wait on Him. "Our soul waiteth for the Lord: he is our help and shield" (Ps. 33:20).

Your strength will be renewed. "But they that wait upon the Lord shall renew their strength; they shall mount up with wings as eagles; they shall run, and not be weary; and they shall walk, and not faint" (Isa. 40:31).

God's promises are fulfilled when we learn to wait on Him. "For the vision is yet for an appointed time, but at the end it shall speak, and not lie: though it tarry, wait for it; because it will surely come, it will not tarry" (Hab. 2:3).

Waiting on God builds up our hope. "I wait for the Lord, my soul doth wait, and in his word do I hope" (Ps. 130:5).

Waiting on God gives us gladness and rejoicing. "And it shall be said in the day, Lo, this is our God; we have waited for him, and he will save us: this is the Lord; we have waited for him, we will be glad and rejoice in his salvation" (Isa. 25:9).

For all of these reasons, and many more, waiting on God has to be a vital part of our prayer life. It is an extremely important prayer key.

Promises to Keep

God keeps all of His promises. We must believe this, pray them, and then simply wait for their fulfillment. C. H. Spurgeon wrote, "Every promise of Scripture is a writing of God, which may be pleaded before Him with this reasonable request: 'Do as Thou hast said.' The Creator will not cheat His creature who depends upon His truth; and, far more, the Heavenly Father will not break His word to His own child. 'Remember the word unto Thy servant, on which Thou hast caused me to hope,' is most prevalent pleading. It is a double argument: It is Thy Word, wilt Thou not keep it? Why hast Thou spoken of it if Thou wilt not make it good? Thou hast caused me to hope in it; wilt Thou disappoint the hope which Thou hast Thyself begotten in me?"

Waiting on God, then, is waiting on Him to fulfill the promises of His Word in our lives. Prayer and the promises go hand in hand as we learn to wait on God.

Waiting Patiently

The Bible says, "As for God, His way is perfect; the word of the Lord is proven; He is a shield to all who trust in Him" (Ps. 18:30, NKJV). All of God's ways are perfect, including His timing. Sometimes we may unwittingly try to get ahead of God by rushing into a situation before the time is right, or by trying to bring something to pass before the appropriate time. Waiting on God involves patience, letting Him have His perfect way.

"Wait on the Lord; be of good courage, and He shall stregthen your heart; wait, I say, on the Lord!" (Ps. 27:14, NKJV). As we learn to wait on God our heart is strengthened and courage is imparted to us.

So many times we are commanded in the Scriptures to wait:

"Wait ye upon Me, saith the Lord, until the day that I rise up to the prey" (Zeph. 3:8).

"Wait for the promise of the Father" (Acts 1:4).

"Ye have need of patience, that, after ye have done the will of God, ye might receive the promise" (Heb. 10:36).

"Let us not be weary in well doing: for in due season we shall reap" (Gal. 6:9).

Waiting on God is an attitude that we must cultivate in prayer, because it is the key to receiving, reaping, strength, courage, and hope. It enhances our faith. It gives us a sense of rest. We are able to wait on the Lord when we fully realize this truth: "One day is with the Lord as a thousand years, and a thousand years as one day" (2 Pet. 3:8).

"I waited patiently for the Lord; and he inclined unto me, and heard my cry" (Ps. 40:1-3).

Waiting Restfully

There is a direct connection between waiting and rest, as the Scriptures point out to us: "Rest in the Lord, and wait patiently for him: fret not thyself because of him who prospereth in his way, because of the man who bringeth wicked devices to pass. Cease from anger, and forsake wrath: fret not thyself in any wise to do evil. For evildoers shall be cut off: but those that wait upon the Lord, they shall inherit the earth" (Ps. 37:7-9).

The earth, in all its fullness, is the rightful inheritance of the children of God as we learn to wait on Him. As we wait restfully in His presence, He gives us wonderful things. The Psalmist points this out: "I waited patiently for the Lord; and he inclined unto me, and heard my cry. He brought me up also out of an horrible pit, out of the miry clay, and set my feet upon a rock, and established my goings. And he hath put a new song in my mouth, even praise unto our God: many shall see it, and fear, and shall trust in the Lord" (Ps. 40:1-3).

As we wait on God in prayer, we can be sure that He is listening to us. This enables us to be hopeful and encouraged in prayer. As we wait on Him, we become more established as believers and this leads us into wider realms of joy and praise. Others will note these changes in our lives, and this will lead many to trust in God.

The saying that all good things come to those who wait was never more true than it is in the life of a praying believer. "And therefore will the Lord wait, that he may be gracious unto you, and therefore will he be exalted, that he may have mercy upon you: for the Lord is a God of judgment: blessed are all they that wait for him" (Isa. 30:18).

Waiting Confidently

As we wait on God patiently and restfully through prayer, we learn to wait on Him with confidence as well. "Therefore I will look unto the Lord; I will wait for the God of my salvation: my God will hear me" (Mic. 7:7).

Our confidence comes from knowing that God will hear us when we wait on Him. Micah expresses the confidence that David described: "Wait on the Lord: be of good courage, and he shall strengthen thine heart: wait, I say, on the Lord" (Ps. 27:14).

Good courage, greater strength, and renewal are promised to those who wait on God. Isaiah wrote, "But they that wait upon the Lord shall renew their strength; they shall mount up with wings as eagles; they shall run, and not be weary; and they shall walk, and not faint" (Isa. 40:31).

Waiting Expectantly

Joyful expectancy is an outgrowth of waiting on God. As we wait on Him we are not just waiting for an answer to our prayer, but we are also waiting for *Him*. He is our life, and He is the answer. It is God that we wait for, as the Psalmist proclaimed: "I wait for the Lord, my soul doth wait, and in his word do I hope. My soul waiteth for the Lord more than they that watch for the morning" (Ps. 130:5-6).

Andrew Murray puts it this way: "Waiting for the answer to prayer is not the whole of waiting, but only a part. . . .When we have special petitions, in connection with which we are waiting on God, our waiting must be very definitely in the confident assurance: 'My God will hear me.' A holy, joyful expectancy is of the very essence of true waiting. And, this is not only true in reference to the many varied requests every believer has to make, but most especially to the one great petition which ought to be the chief thing every heart seeks for itself – that the life of God in the soul may have full sway. That Christ may be fully formed within, and that we may be filled to all the fullness of God."

Let our attitude be, "My soul, wait only upon God." This is faith in action, and it is a style of prayer that God will hear. Our continual prayer should be: "Show me thy ways, O Lord; teach me thy paths. Lead me in thy truth, and teach me: for thou art the God of my salvation; on thee do I wait all the day" (Ps. 25:4-5).

As we wait upon Him, may we experience His wonderful presence. May we say with the Psalmist, "In thy presence is fulness of joy" (Ps. 16:11).

Prayer of Application

Upon you only, Lord God, will I wait.[1] You are my wonderful Father, and I rejoice in your perfect way.[2] I know your way is perfect, your Word is proven, and you will be a mighty shield for me.[3] Thank you, Father.

How I praise you for your exceedingly great and precious promises that enable me to partake of your nature and to escape the corruption that is in this world.[4] I rest in you,

Lord God, and I wait patiently for you, because I know that those who wait upon you will inherit the earth,[5] and never be ashamed.[6]

Show me your ways and teach me your paths. Lead me in your truth and teach me, for you are the God of my salvation, and I wait on you all day long.[7] Let integrity and uprightness preserve me as I wait on you, Father.[8]

Thank you for always being good to me.[9] I will ever seek you as I hope in you and wait patiently for you.[10] My expectation is from you, Father, because I recognize you to be my rock and my salvation. You are my defense, and because I know this is true, I know I shall never be moved.[11]

My hope is in you, mighty God. Deliver me from all my transgressions. Don't let me ever become a reproach of the foolish.[12] How I thank you for the realization that people since the beginning of the world have neither seen nor heard all that you have prepared for those who wait upon you.[13] With your help, Father, I will be a person who waits on you confidently, restfully, and expectantly, knowing that you will reveal all good things to me.

Thank you, Father.

References: (1) Psalms 62:1; (2) Psalms 18:30; (3) Psalms 18:30; (4) 2 Peter 1:4; (5) Psalms 37:7-9; (6) Psalms 25:3-5; (7) Psalms 25:3-5; (8) Psalms 25:21; (9) Lamentations

8
KEY # 8 – THANKSGIVING AND PRAISE

Know ye that the Lord he is God: it is
he that hath made us, and not we
ourselves; we are his people, and the
sheep of his pasture. Enter into his
gates with thanksgiving, and into
his courts with praise: be thankful
unto him, and bless his name.
(Ps. 100:3-4)

Thanksgiving Is Thanks-Living

Jeremy Taylor wrote, "The private and personal blessings we enjoy, the blessings of protection, safeguard, liberty, and integrity, deserve the thanksgiving of a whole life." Thanksgiving is not just a date on a calendar, it is a life style. Paul wrote, "Rejoice evermore. Pray without ceasing. In every thing give thanks: for this is the will of God in Christ Jesus concerning you" (1 Thess. 5:16-18).

What is God's will for you? He wants you to learn to give thanks in everything. This does not necessarily mean, however, that we give thanks *for* everything that happens, but that our hearts are set in the direction of thanksgiving at all times, no matter what circumstances we may be passing through.

In the midst of everything, God wants us to be encouraged and pray with a heart of thanksgiving. When things are going well we give Him thanks for His blessings and goodness. When the storms of life come and things are going badly, we give Him thanks for His faithfulness because we are confident that He will take care of us.

Earlier we looked at the powerful prayer promise in 1 John 5:14-15: "Now this is the confidence that we have in Him, that if we ask anything according to His will, He hears us. And if we know that He hears us, whatever we ask, we know that we have the petitions that we have asked of Him" (NKJV). Since we know it is God's will for us to give thanks in everything, it is clear that every thankful prayer is in accord with God's will for us, and He promises to hear our prayer of thanksgiving.

Thanksgiving is not just a flow of words; it is a way of living that stems from faith and may express many positive emotions. The Psalmist writes, "It is a good thing to give thanks unto the Lord" (Ps. 92:1). It is good in more ways than one. First and foremost, it blesses God. Secondly, it blesses us. Thirdly, it opens the gates that lead into His presence, and this is where we always want to be. We enter the gates of God with thanksgiving, and we go into His presence through praise.

John Henry Jowett wrote, "Life without thankfulness is devoid of love and passion. Hope without thankfulness is lacking in fine perception. Faith without thankfulness lacks strength and fortitude. Every virtue divorced from thankfulness is maimed and limps along the spiritual road."

Promises of Praise and Thanksgiving

We are often commanded to praise God for all the wonderful things He does for us. Notice what happens when we do:

"Because thy lovingkindness is better than life, my lips shall praise thee. Thus will I bless thee while I live: I will lift up my hands in thy name. My soul shall be satisfied as with marrow and fatness; and my mouth shall praise thee with joyful lips" (Ps. 63:3-5).

"Whoso offereth praise glorifieth me: and to him that ordereth his conversation aright will I shew the salvation of God" (Ps. 50:23).

"But ye are a chosen generation, a royal priesthood, an holy nation, a peculiar people; that ye should shew forth the praises of him who hath called you out of darkness into his marvellous light" (1 Pet. 2:9).

"O give thanks unto the God of heaven: for his mercy endureth for ever" (Ps. 136:26).

"For every creature of God is good, and nothing to be refused, if it be received with thanksgiving" (1 Tim. 4:4).

"Be careful for nothing; but in every thing by prayer and supplication with thanksgiving let your requests be made known unto God" (Phil. 4:6).

The prayer key of thanksgiving and praise is one that helps us in so many ways. It gives us satisfaction. It glorifies God and brings revelation of His wonderful salvation. It shows that we've been called out of darkness into God's marvelous light. It helps us to see that God's mercy endures forever, and it enables us to receive all the good things God has provided for us. In addition, it eradicates all anxiety from our lives.

Fanny Crosby wrote hundreds of hymns which have stirred the Church of Jesus Christ for many years. She became blind as a little girl due to a doctor's surgical error. She once said, "I have heard that this physician never ceased expressing his regret at the occurrence [the mistake that resulted in her blindness]; and that it was one of the sorrows of his life. But if I could meet him now, I would say, 'Thank you, thank you, over and over again.'"

Fanny's thankfulness stemmed from her belief that she might not have been so effectively used by God as a hymn writer if the blindness had not occurred. She went on, ". . .that I should live my days in physical darkness, so as to be better prepared to sing His praises and incite others to do so."

Fanny Crosby learned the importance of praise and thanksgiving early in life, for at the age of eight she penned these lines:

> Oh, what a happy soul am I!
> Though blind and cannot see.
> I am resolved that in this world,
> Contented I will be.

What an inspiring example she has given to us both in her testimony and her songs.

Pray With Thanksgiving

It is essential for us to pray with thanksgiving. When we reflect upon our lives we see how often God has intervened to answer our prayers, bless us, heal us, use us, and keep us time after time. He is our awesome God of faithfulness, and this fact alone should cultivate an attitude of gratitude in our hearts. If thankfulness is the attitude of our hearts it will automatically come out in our prayers.

How many times has God answered your prayers? How many miracles has He given to you? How has His ministry in your life changed you? What has He done for members of your family? How has He led you? As you take a look at these things, you will find that your heart will swell with thanksgiving to the God who does all things well.

It is clear that God wants us to express our thanks to Him. As Jesus was traveling in the region between Samaria and Galilee He encountered ten lepers. They asked Him for healing, and the Master granted their request. Jesus then commanded them to show their cleansing to the priests. Only one of them (a Samaritan), however, returned to Jesus in order to thank Him for his healing. This man glorified God with a loud voice and fell on his face at the feet of Jesus, giving Him thanks.

Jesus responded to this man with happiness, but he expressed sadness and disappointment over the fact that the other nine men whom He had healed had not returned with gratitude. He said, "Were there not ten cleansed? But where are the nine? Were there not any found who returned to give glory to God except this foreigner? . . . Arise, go your way. Your faith has made you well" (Luke 17:17-19, NKJV).

God wants us to tell Him how thankful we are for all that He does for us.

Try this little exercise. Get off somewhere alone where you can pray without interruptions. Then sit or kneel before God, close your eyes, and be still. Maintain this attitude of quiet prayer. As you do this, let your heart connect with God, and let God connect with you. If you will do this in faith, believing that God loves you and wants to spend time with you, He will bless you with the joy of His presence.

Thanksgiving Builds Our Faith

As we thankfully review God's accomplishments in and through us, our faith in Him continues to grow. It helps us to go to God with a greater sense of assurance, because we know how He has heard us and acted upon our prayers in the past.

When we realize how much God has blessed us, we have great faith to receive more from His hands. In fact, we begin to look expectantly for answers to our prayers so that we can thank Him again and again.

King David knew this truth, and he became a strong man of prayer and thanksgiving. The Psalms are filled with thanksgiving and praise, such as the following:

"But let all those that put their trust in thee rejoice: let them ever shout for joy, because thou defendest them: let them also that love thy name be joyful in thee" (Ps. 5:11).

"I will praise thee, O Lord, with my whole heart; I will shew forth all thy marvellous works. I will be glad and rejoice in thee: I will sing praise to thy name, O thou most High" (Ps. 9:1-2).

"I will sing unto the Lord, because he hath dealt bountifully with me" (Ps. 13:6).

"I will call upon the Lord, who is worthy to be praised: so shall I be saved from mine enemies" (Ps. 18:3).

"Therefore will I give thanks unto thee, O Lord, among the heathen, and sing praises unto thy name" (Ps. 18:49).

"I will declare thy name unto my brethren: in the midst of the congregation will I praise thee" (Ps. 22:22).

"Give unto the Lord the glory due unto his name; worship the Lord in the beauty of holiness" (Ps. 29:2).

"Be glad in the Lord, and rejoice, ye righteous: and shout for joy all ye that are upright in heart" (Ps. 32:11).

"Rejoice in the Lord, O ye righteous: for praise is comely for the upright" (Ps. 33:1).

"I will bless the Lord at all times: his praise shall continually be in my mouth" (Ps. 34:1).

"I will give thanks in the great congregation: I will praise thee among much people" (Ps. 35:18).

"I waited patiently for the Lord; and he inclined unto me, and heard my cry. He brought me up also out of an horrible pit, out of the miry clay, and set my feet upon a rock, and established my goings. And he hath put a new song in my mouth, even praise unto our God: many shall see it, and fear, and shall trust in the Lord" (Ps. 40:1-3).

"Whoso offereth praise glorifieth me: and to him that ordereth his conversation aright will I shew the salvation of God" (Ps. 50:23).

David's heart was set on praising God. As he pondered God's mighty acts in his life, his faith mushroomed, and he was able to reach out to God for more. The same will happen in each believer's life as they set their will to praise God at all times and in all things.

The apostles were much like David in their desire to praise God at all times and in all situations:

"And they worshipped him, and returned to Jerusalem with great joy: And were continually in the temple, praising and blessing God" (Luke 24:52-53).

"And they, continuing daily with one accord in the temple, and breaking bread from house to house, did eat their meat with gladness and singleness of heart. Praising God, and having favour with all the people. And the Lord added to the church daily such as should be saved" (Acts 2:46-47).

"And at midnight Paul and Silas prayed, and sang praises unto God: and the prisoners heard them" (Acts 16:25).

"But ye are a chosen generation, a royal priesthood, an holy nation, a peculiar people; that ye should shew forth the praises of him who hath called you out of darkness into his marvellous light" (1 Pet. 2:9).

"Speaking to yourselves in psalms and hymns and spiritual songs, singing and making melody in your heart to the Lord. Giving thanks always for all things unto God and the Father in the name of our Lord Jesus Christ" (Eph. 5:19-20).

Let Your Requests Be Made Known With Thanksgiving

It is thankful praying that keeps us from anxiety, because such praying is rooted in faith. Paul told the Colossians: "Continue in prayer, and watch in the same with thanksgiving" (Col. 4:2). All of our praying should emanate from a thankful heart.

We can be thankful both for what God has already done, and for all that we trust Him to do in response to our requests. God, our Father, responds to the thankful hearts of His children.

Thankfulness is the only appropriate response to God when we realize the truth of His promises. Read the following passage from Deuteronomy and see what effect it has on your thankfulness quotient:

"And it shall come to pass, if thou shalt hearken diligently unto the voice of the Lord thy God, to observe and to do all his commandments which I command thee this day, that the Lord thy God will set thee on high above all nations of the earth: And all these blessings shall come on thee, and overtake thee, if thou shalt hearken unto the voice of the Lord thy God. Blessed shalt thou be in the city, and blessed shalt thou be in the field. Blessed shall be the fruit of thy body, and the fruit of thy ground, and the fruit of thy cattle, the increase of thy kine, and the flocks of thy sheep. Blessed shall be thy basket and thy store. Blessed shalt thou be when thou comest in, and blessed shalt thou be when thou goest out. . . . The Lord shall command the blessing upon thee in thy storehouses, and in all that thou settest thine hand unto; and he shall bless thee in the land which the Lord thy God giveth thee. . . . And the Lord shall make thee plenteous in goods, in the fruit of thy body, and in the fruit of thy cattle, and in the fruit of thy ground, in the land which the Lord sware unto thy fathers to give thee. The Lord shall open unto thee his good treasure, the heaven to give the rain unto thy land in his season, and to bless all the work of thine hand: and thou shalt lend unto many nations, and thou shalt not borrow. And the Lord shall make thee the head, and not the tail; and thou shalt be above only, and thou shalt not be beneath; if thou hearken unto the commandments of the Lord thy God, which I command thee this day, to observe and to do them" (Deut. 28:1-13).

Those who believe these promises from God are the happiest and most thankful people on earth because they know:

God will set them on high.

God's blessings will come on them and overtake them.

God will bless them in the city and in the field.

God will bless the fruit of their bodies and their ground.

God will bless their supplies.

God will bless them when they go in and when they come out.

God will command a blessing upon them and their storehouses.

God will bless all that they set their hand to.

God will bless them in the land that He gives to them.

God will make them plenteous in goods.

God will open His good treasure to them.

God will make them the head, not the tail.

God will put them above only, and not underneath.

All of these wonderful things will happen to those who put their trust in God and obey His commandments, one of which is coming to Him with a thankful heart. As we count our blessings, we are filled with gratitude which spills over into our prayers and praise.

E.M. Bounds writes, "Giving thanks is the very life of prayer. It is its fragrance and music, its poetry and its crown. Prayer bringing the desired answer breaks out into praise and thanksgiving. So that whatever interferes with and injures the spirit of prayer necessarily hurts and dissipates the spirit of praise."

A woman who was going through the stresses surrounding her pending divorce from her husband of twenty years went to her pastor for counseling. He said, "There's only one thing I know to do, and that's to get on your knees and start thanking and praising God, not for the prospect of divorce, but for all that He's doing in your life."

At first, the lady was shocked at such seemingly callous advice. She protested, "What do I have to thank God for?"

"That's just the problem," the pastor replied. "You need to get your focus off of the bad things that are happening, and look at the many positives in your life. You have your health, your career, your children, your home, and so many other things. Most importantly, though, you have your relationship with your heavenly Father."

He paused, and then once again suggested, "Let's get on our knees and start praising God."

The pastor and his parishioner began to express praise and thanksgiving to God both for who He is and for all He was doing. This went on for half an hour. The woman began to sob. Her tears were tears of repentance, and she began to realize how she had failed in her relationship with her husband. Always before, she could only see his faults, and not her own.

This experience, resulting from praise and thanksgiving, caused her to rethink many things about her life. She went to her husband, sought his forgiveness, and pledged to be a better wife to him. He, in turn, forgave her, and sought her forgiveness for failing her in so many ways. Their marriage was restored, and this couple eventually went on to serve God on the mission field.

Praise and thanksgiving change so many things in our lives. We learn to count our blessings instead of listing our problems. We become God-centered instead of problem-centered. We experience joy instead of depression, and many things in our lives begin to change as our perspective changes.

Prayer of Application

O God, you are so great, and you are greatly to be praised.[1] I praise you and thank you for all these blessings in my life:

_____

_____

_____

_____.

Thank you for everything, Father, especially for the great and precious promises of your Word which enrich my life so fully.[2] You have shown your greatness and your mighty hand to me time after time.[3] You are my rock and my fortress and my deliverer. You are the God of my strength, and I will always trust in you. You are my shield and the horn of my salvation. You are my stronghold and my refuge. You are my Savior.[4] Thank you, Father, for being my awesome God.

I gladly give thanks to you as I call upon your name. Help me to make your deeds known among the people around me.[5] I love to give thanks to you, Lord God, for I know how good you are to me. Your wonderful mercies endure forever.[6]

I will praise you with all of my heart, Father. I will tell others of your marvelous works. I am truly glad, and I rejoice in you. Therefore, I will ever sing praises to your name, O Most High.[7] I bless you, Father. All that is within me blesses your holy name. I will never forget all your benefits to me. You forgive all my iniquities. You heal all my diseases. You have redeemed my life from destruction. You crown me with your lovingkindness and your tender mercies. You satisfy my mouth with good things, and you renew my youth.[8] Thank you for everything, wonderful Father.

References: *(1) Psalms 48:1-2; (2) 2 Peter 1:4; (3) Deuteronomy 3:24; (4) 2 Samuel 22:2-3; (5) 1 Chronicles 16:8-12; (6) 1 Chronicles 16:34; (7) Psalms 9:2; (8) Psalms 103:1-5.*

REMEMBER THIS: **IT SHOULDN'T BE WHAT WE HAVE IN OUR HANDS OR OUR POCKETS THAT MAKES US THANKFUL, BUT IT IS WHO GOD IS AND WHAT WE HAVE IN OUR HEARTS THAT SHOULD MAKE US THANKFUL.**

9

KEY # 9 – ABIDING IN CHRIST

*Abide in Me, and I in you. As the
branch cannot bear fruit of itself, unless
it abides in the vine, neither can you,
unless you abide in Me. I am the vine,
you are the branches. He who abides
in Me, and I in him, bears much fruit;
for without Me you can do nothing.*
(John 15:4-5, NKJV)

Staying Put

There are at least three definitions for the
word *abiding*. One has to do with waiting,
which we have covered in an earlier chapter.
The second denotation of the word involves
remaining stable or fixed. The third meaning
relates to continuing in a given place or
dwelling.

Certainly all three of these explanations
relate to our need for abiding in Christ. We
watch and wait in Him as we become stable
and fixed in our resolve to remain in and with
Him. Abiding in Christ is continuing in Him
and in His love.

This constant abiding is a foundational key
in the life of prayer. Oswald Chambers writes:
"It is the dull, bald, dreary, commonplace day,

with commonplace duties and people, that kills the burning heart unless we have learned the secret of abiding in Jesus."

Jesus is our safe place, our refuge from the storms of life; but the key to getting our prayers answered is not found in fleeing to Jesus when the times get rough – this key only works when we learn to live in Him, to stay there, knowing that He is our true abode (dwelling-place), our resting place, our home. In Him we live and move and have our being. (See Acts 17:28.) In Him all things find their completion, and in Him all things hold together. (See Col. 1:16-17.) Because these things are true, we can be certain that abiding in Christ will bring answers to our prayers.

Abiding is staying put, and this is an important key to answered prayer.

The Power of Abiding

As we have seen, abiding in Christ entails waiting, persevering, enduring, keeping on keeping on, staying put, withstanding, bearing patiently, and staying fixed. To abide in Christ, therefore, is to remain in Him and to wait patiently on Him. Abiding in Him is the best of all places to be. He is our dwelling place and we are His abode.

We must abide in Christ and in the Father, as the Apostle John points out: "Therefore let that abide in you which you heard from the beginning. If what you heard from the beginning abides in you, you also will abide in the Son and in the Father. And this is the promise that He has promised us – eternal life. These things I have written to you concerning those who try to deceive you. But the anointing which you have received from Him abides in you, and you do not need that anyone teach you; but as the same anointing teaches you concerning all things, and is true, and is not a lie, and just as it has taught you, you will abide in Him. And now, little children, abide in Him, that when He appears, we may have confidence and not be ashamed before Him at His coming" (1 John 2:24-28, NKJV).

By abiding in Christ, and letting His words abide in us, we shall be able to ask what we will, and it shall be done. This opens the way for the Holy Spirit's anointing to bless our prayers and actions, and we will become fruitful. We will remember the things that Jesus has taught us, and we will not be ashamed when He returns.

One important key to abiding in Christ is obedience. John writes: "Now he who keeps His commandments abides in Him, and He in him. And by this we know that He abides in us, by the Spirit whom He has given us" (1 John 3:24, NKJV).

Andrew Murray explains, "The main thought is permanent, steadfast, and immovable continuance in the place and the blessing secured to us in Christ and God. The great secret of the world is its transitoriness – it passes away with all its glory. And all who are of it partake of its vanity and uncertainty. And just as far as the Christian breathes its spirit and allows its love a place in his heart, he loses the power of abiding."

Christ Is Our All

Dwight L. Moody once discovered among his papers a powerful quotation about the person of Christ. He was unable to determine who had penned it, but its compelling images give us great insights into abiding in Christ: "Christ is our Way; we walk in Him. He is our truth; we embrace Him. He is our Life; we live in Him. He is our Lord; we choose Him to rule over us. He is our Master; we serve Him. He is our Teacher, instructing us in the way of salvation. He is our Prophet, pointing out the future. He is our Priest, having atoned for us. He is our Advocate, ever living to make intercession for us. He is our Savior, saving to the uttermost. He is our Root; we grow from Him. He is our Bread; we feed upon Him. He is our Shepherd, leading us into green pastures. He is our true Vine; we abide in Him. He is the Water of Life; we satisfy our thirst from Him. He is the fairest among the thousand; we admire Him above all others. He is 'the brightness of the Father's glory, and the express image of His person.' We strive to reflect His likeness. He is the upholder of all things; we rest upon Him. He is our wisdom; we are guided by Him. He is our Righteousness; we cast all our imperfections upon Him. He is our Sanctification; we draw all our power for holy life from Him. He is our Redemption, redeeming us from all iniquity. He is our Healer, curing all our diseases. He is our Friend, relieving us in all our necessities. He is our Brother, cheering us in our difficulties."

To abide in Christ, then, is to abide in all these marvelous truths. Jesus is all in all to us. He has chosen to take up His abode in our hearts, and we are invited to take up our abode within His heart. He is in us, and we are in Him.

Fruitful Believers

Jesus chose us so that we would become fruitful believers in His family. John wrote down these words of Jesus: "You did not choose Me, but I chose you and appointed you that you should go and bear fruit, and that your fruit should remain, that whatever you ask the Father in My name He may give you" (John 15:16, NKJV).

Such fruitfulness, the Master already pointed out, stems from abiding in Him and letting His words abide in us. He explained, ". . . .without Me you can do nothing" (John 15:5, NKJV).

Notice what happens when we abide in Him: "If you abide in Me, and My words abide in you, you will ask what you desire, and it shall be done for you. By this My Father is glorified, that you bear much fruit; so you will be My disciples" (John 15:7-8, NKJV).

As we abide in Christ, and let His words abide in us, we become fruitful believers in every area of our lives, including prayer. Jesus said He chose us to be fruitful so that: ". . .whatever you ask the Father in My name He may give you" (John 15:16, NKJV).

These are wonderful prayer promises associated with abiding in Christ, and they are as true today as they were when Jesus first spoke them. God, the Father, will hear us when we are abiding in Christ, and He will bring answers to our prayers.

Branches on the Vine

A branch has no life of its own. It is totally dependent on the vine for its nurturance and continuance. Sometimes the vinedresser needs to trim the branches so that they will be even closer to the vine in order to assure their continued fruitfulness. The same is true with every believer.

We have no life apart from Jesus. The heavenly Father, our vinedresser, has grafted us into the vine of His Son, Jesus. He prunes us so that we will get ever closer to the vine and become ever more fruitful.

In order to abide in Christ, therefore, we must give up any right to self-determination. He has redeemed us and we are not our own. We belong to Him. We have become part and parcel with Christ, and His life flows through us. It is in Him, and through His life, that we get the spiritual nutrients we need to keep going on. This is how we fulfill our destiny— God's personal plan for us.

As this becomes a reality in our life, the prayers we pray are no longer composed of our own thoughts and ideas, but in a very real sense, the mind of Christ is praying through us. This is why the Father promises to hear and answer our prayers when we abide in Christ.

The Words of Jesus

Jesus wants us to abide in Him, and He wants His words to abide in us. This is because His words are ". . .spirit, and they are life" (John 6:63, NKJV). We need to hide the Word of God in our hearts, as the Psalmist pointed out: "How can a young man cleanse his way? By taking heed according to Your word. With my whole heart I have sought You; Oh, let me not wander from Your commandments! Your word have I hidden in my heart, that I might not sin against You. Blessed are You, O Lord! Teach me Your statutes" (Ps. 119:9-12, NKJV).

Abiding in Christ includes letting the Word of God take root in our hearts. The Word is a great source of power in prayer, because it is, ". . .living and powerful, and sharper than any two-edged sword, piercing even to the division of soul and spirit, and of joints and marrow, and is a discerner of the thoughts and intents of the heart" (Heb. 4:12, NKJV).

The words of Christ, and the Word of God, become the skeletal matter of our prayers which we then flesh out with our personal requests and concerns. As we pray the Word, God listens carefully, and He quickly moves to meet our need.

R. A. Torrey writes, "The prayer that is born of meditation on the Word of God is the prayer which soars upward to God's listening ear. George Mueller, one of the mightiest men of prayer, would begin praying by reading and meditating upon God's Word until a prayer began to form itself in his heart. Thus, God Himself was the real author of prayer, and God answered the prayer which He Himself had inspired."

Abiding in Christ, and letting His words abide in us, is, therefore, a powerful key to answered prayer. Paul wrote, "Let the word of Christ dwell in you richly in all wisdom; teaching and admonishing one another in psalms and hymns and spiritual songs, singing with grace in your hearts to the Lord" (Col. 3:16).

Abiding in Love

Abiding in Christ is abiding in His love. Jesus said, "As the Father loved Me, I also have loved you; abide in My love. If you keep My commandments, you will abide in My love, just as I have kept My Father's commandments and abide in His love. These things I have spoken to you, that My joy may remain in you, and that your joy may be full" (John 15:9-11, NKJV).

As we learn to abide in Christ and let His words abide in us, we will experience His love in new and wonderful ways. The result will be great and full joy as we see God answering our prayers and showing us His ways.

John wrote, "But whoso keepeth his word, in him verily is the love of God perfected: hereby know we that we are in him. He that saith he abideth in him ought himself also so to walk, even as he walked" (1 John 2:5-6).

In *The Wonderful Wizard of Oz* Dorothy desperately wanted to return home to Kansas after she had experienced a bit of the terrors of Oz. To her, there was no place like home. The same is true for every believer, there is no place like home. The true vine of Jesus Christ is our home; it is the place where we were meant to be.

Prayer of Application

Heavenly Father, thank you for loving the world so much that you sent your only begotten Son. I believe in Him, and I know I have eternal life.[1] How I rejoice in your so great salvation, mighty God.[2]

Thank you for Jesus who is the way, the truth, and the life to me.[3] With your help, I will abide in Him and I will let His words abide in me so that you will hear me when I pray and fulfill my requests.[4] Thank you for this powerful promise from your Word.

I praise you, Lord God, for grafting me into the living vine of Jesus Christ, my Lord.[5] Through Him, you have chosen me to bear lasting fruit,[6] and because this is true I know that the things I ask for in prayer, Father, will be accomplished as I abide in Christ.[7] As an abiding, fruitful Christian, I know that I will not be ashamed when Jesus returns. When He reappears I will have the confidence that comes from abiding in Him.[8]

Help me always to delight myself in your statutes, Father, so that I will never forget your Word.[9] Through your grace, I will let your Word dwell richly within me,[10] because I know it is a lamp unto my feet, and a light unto my path.[11] It's wonderful to know that abiding in Christ, and letting His words abide in me, will keep me from sin.[12] Thank you, Lord God.

Throughout my life, with your help, I will abide in Christ, and walk in Him and in His Word.[13] Even now, as I draw near to you, Father, I know you are drawing near to me.[14] Thank you so much.

References: (1) John 3:16; (2) Hebrews 2:3; (3) John 14:6; (4) John 15:7; (5) Romans 11:23; (6) John 15:7; (7) John 15:7-8; (8) 1 John 2:28; (9) Psalms 119:16; (10) Colossians 3:16; (11) Psalms 119:105; (12) 1 John 3:6; (13) John 15:7; (14) James 4:8.

REMEMBER THIS: TO ABIDE IN CHRIST IS TO STAY PUT, NOT EVER LETTING ANYTHING MOVE YOU ASIDE. THIS IS A VERY POWERFUL KEY TO ANSWERED PRAYER.

10

KEY # 10 – ABSOLUTE SURRENDER

And he said to them all, If any man will come after me, let him deny himself, and take up his cross daily, and follow me. For whosoever will save his life shall lose it: but whosoever will lose his life for my sake, the same shall save it. For what is a man advantaged, if he gain the whole world, and lose himself, or be cast away?
(Luke 9:23-25)

Who Is the Lord of Your Life?

A lord, in earthly terms, is one who has authority over his particular domain. In medieval times, a lord would have been in charge of a particular fief or feud, and everyone who lived on that property would have been subject to him.

The servants or vassals of a lord are expected to do exactly what he says, to obey him and serve him with all that they are and have. In return, the lord supplies them with all their needs.

In effect, these servants are like slaves of their master. They have surrendered their personal rights and interests to the one who provides for them. It is the same in the spiritual realm. Jesus is our Lord and Master. As His servants, we need to surrender everything into His Lordship. He promises to bless us when we absolutely surrender everything to Him.

Andrew Murray writes, "The condition for obtaining God's full blessing is *absolute surrender*."

Paul writes, "And my God shall supply all your need according to His riches in glory by Christ Jesus" (Phil. 4:19, NKJV).

God has bought us with a terrible price – the death of His dear Son. Paul describes it this way: "You were bought at a price. Therefore honor God with your body" (1 Cor. 6:20, NIV).

God's abundant mercies to us demand our absolute surrender to Him. "I beseech you therefore, brethren, by the mercies of God, that you present your bodies a living sacrifice, holy, acceptable to God, which is your reasonable service. And do not be conformed to this world, but be transformed by the renewing of your mind, that you may prove what is that good and acceptable and perfect will of God" (Rom. 12:1-2, NKJV).

Are you willing to surrender yourself completely to the Lordship of Jesus Christ? If you do, God is ready to hear and answer your prayers. He will reveal His will to you, and you will be able to pray accordingly.

Friends of Jesus

Jesus said, "This is My commandment, that you love one another as I have loved you. Greater love has no one than this, than to lay down one's life for his friends. You are My friends if you do whatever I command you. No longer do I call you servants, for a servant does not know what his master is doing; but I have called you friends, for all things that I heard from My Father I have made known to you. You did not choose Me, but I chose you and appointed you that you should go and bear fruit, and that your fruit should remain, that whatever you ask the Father in My name He may give you" (John 15:12-16, NKJV).

Jesus is our Lord, but He desires a close personal relationship with each of us. In fact, He desires us to be His friends. In such an intimate, caring relationship many wonderful things transpire, but the first step, as Jesus points out, is laying down our lives for Him.

As His servants, we must surrender all aspects of self-determination to Him. He is our Lord and Master. His will is what counts.

As we learn to surrender everything to Him, God promises to answer our prayers. Yielding totally to Him allows Him to work in us and bring our wills into agreement with Him. Our prayers become powerful when they are in agreement with God's will.

Surrendering our lives to God implies an absolute surrender to His will and a firm belief that He always knows what's best for us. Jesus modeled this attitude of surrender for us when He prayed so fervently in the Garden of Gethsemane: "Father, if you are willing, take this cup from me; yet not my will, but yours, be done" (Luke 22:42, NIV).

God expects your complete surrender. He will help you to take the leap of faith that such an absolute surrender requires. Your surrendered heart will become a prized possession of His, and He will enable you to maintain this relationship to Him as He blesses you with answers to your prayers!

Serve God With All Your Heart and Soul

Joshua knew about absolute surrender. He wrote, "But take diligent heed to do the commandment and the law, which Moses the servant of the Lord charged you, to love the Lord your God, and to walk in all his ways, and to keep his commandments, and to cleave unto him, and to serve him with all your heart and with all your soul" (Josh. 22:5).

Heed God's commandments. Love God. Walk in His ways, and keep His commandments. Cleave unto God, and serve Him with all your heart and all your soul. These are the active components of absolute surrender, and God expects no less from each of us.

Notice what happens when we thusly surrender our lives to Him: "And ye shall serve the Lord your God, and he shall bless thy bread, and thy water; and I will take sickness away from the midst of thee. There shall nothing cast their young, nor be barren, in thy land: the number of thy days I will fulfil" (Exod. 23:25-26).

The same sentiment is expressed in Deuteronomy: "And it shall come to pass, if ye shall hearken diligently unto my commandments which I command you this day, to love the Lord your God, and to serve him with all your heart and with all your soul, that I will give you the rain of your land in his due season, the first rain and the latter rain, that thou mayest gather in thy corn, and thy wine, and thine oil. And I will send grass in thy fields for thy cattle, that thou mayest eat and be full" (Deut. 11:13-15).

Jesus picks up this very important theme in the gospels. He talks about the importance of obeying His commandments, and He concludes with several prayer promises. He said, "Most assuredly, I say to you, whatever you ask the Father in My name He will give you. Until now you have asked nothing in My name. Ask, and you will receive, that your joy may be full" (John 16:23-24, NKJV).

Surrender of Love to Love

Our surrender relates directly to the first commandment: "And you shall love the Lord your God with all your heart, with all your soul, with all your mind, and with all your strength" (Mark 12:30, NKJV). Absolute surrender, therefore, involves a choice on our part. We choose to obey His command to love Him totally and completely with all of our being.

Most of us feel inadequate to love Him in this way, but this is where His grace comes in. As we commit our complete and total love to Him, He imparts grace that enables us to grow in loving Him.

John writes, "We love Him because He first loved us" (1 John 4:19, NKJV). In Romans we read, "Now hope does not disappoint, because the love of God has been poured out in our hearts by the Holy Spirit who was given to us" (Rom. 5:5, NKJV).

As children of God, new creatures in Christ, we have been set free and enabled to begin this great walk of love. Throughout Church history Christians have felt inadequate to love God completely. Yet, the command is there and the promise of His sustaining and enabling help still stands.

Is it possible for us to love God like this? Emphatically, yes! The secret is absolute surrender. God the Holy Spirit has come to dwell within our hearts. One of the loveliest facets of His ministry is to produce His fruit of love in our lives.

Paul tells us that the first of the fruit of the Spirit is love. As we surrender to God and ask Him to grow the fruit of love in us, He will do it. We can rest assured in faith, knowing this is the perfect will of God for each of us.

The beautiful thing about it is that He commands us to do it and then He provides the grace to fulfill it. Isn't that just like Him? He is our wonderful Heavenly Father. He loves us with an everlasting love. Truly our lives can be a surrender of love to Love.

Meditation in God's Word

One who is absolutely surrendered to God is able to claim the promises of His Word. Joshua wrote, "This book of the law shall not depart out of thy mouth; but thou shalt meditate therein day and night, that thou mayest observe to do according to all that is written therein: for then thou shalt make thy way prosperous, and then thou shalt have good success" (Josh. 1:8).

Prosperity and good success are promised to the surrendered soul who has given full heed to the Word of God, and continually meditates upon its precepts. This truth is echoed in Psalms: "Blessed is the man that walketh not in the counsel of the ungodly, nor standeth in the way of sinners, nor sitteth in the seat of the scornful. But his delight is in the law of the Lord; and in his law doth he meditate day and night. And he shall be like a tree planted by the rivers of water, that bringeth forth his fruit in his season; his leaf also shall not wither; and whatsoever he doeth shall prosper" (Ps. 1:1-3).

The key to success in the Kingdom of God is found in surrender, not in self-promotion and self-aggrandizement.

Obedience

When I surrender my rights to another, I am expected to fulfill the other's wishes, to obey their commands. The same is true in the spiritual life. God expects me to obey Him, and absolute surrender absolutely entails full compliance with His rules, regulations, and wishes, realizing that He has given these edicts to keep me safe and happy. They provide direction and boundaries on the pathway of His will for my life.

He promises, "If you are willing and obedient, you shall eat the good of the land" (Isa. 1:19, NKJV).

This involves the surrender of our wills. Jesus said, "Not everyone that saith unto me, Lord, Lord, shall enter into the kingdom of heaven; but he that doeth the will of my Father which is in heaven" (Matt. 7:21).

Jesus set the example of absolute surrender and obedience for us: "My meat is to do the will of him that sent me, and to finish his work" (John 4:34).

Paul tells us to be like Jesus: "Let each of you look out not only for his own interests, but also for the interests of others. Let this mind be in you which was also in Christ Jesus, who, being in the form of God, did not consider it robbery to be equal with God, but made Himself of no reputation, taking the form of a bondservant, and coming in the likeness of men. And being found in appearance as a man, He humbled Himself and became obedient to the point of death, even the death of the cross. Therefore God also has highly exalted Him and given Him the name which is above every name, that at the name of Jesus every knee should bow, of those in heaven, and of those on earth, and of those under the earth, and that every tongue should confess that Jesus Christ is Lord, to the glory of God the Father" (Phil. 2:4-11, NKJV).

Jesus surrendered His position in heaven, and His very life, for us. Therefore, it is imperative that we surrender our lives to Him, in total obedience to His will.

Some might consider it to be a paradox, but true freedom in the Kingdom of God comes by way of absolute surrender and obedience. "For God is not unrighteous to forget your work and labor of love which you have shown toward His name, in that you have ministered to the saints, and do minister" (Heb. 6:10, NKJV).

Andrew Murray writes, "The key to God's blessing is absolute surrender of all into His hands. Praise God! If our hearts are willing for that, there is no end to what God will do for us, and to the blessing God will bestow."

The great Welsh Revival of 1904 brought repentance and salvation to thousands of villagers throughout the country. It was a revival that was birthed in prayer. As God moved on the hearts of people in all walks of life, including coal miners, farmers, and businesspeople, they gave their lives in absolute surrender to Him.

As a result, many experienced untold blessings, including miracles, that they had never known or seen before. The key was absolute surrender to the Lordship of Christ. A Chicago newspaper described the revival this way: "A wonderful revival is sweeping over Wales. The whole country, from the city to the colliery underground, is aflame with gospel glory. Police courts are hardly necessary, public houses are being deserted, old debts are being paid to satisfy awakened consciences, and definite and unmistakable answers to prayer are recorded."

Let's pray for such a heaven-borne revival to sweep the world today. Amazing things always happen when people surrender their lives to God. He responds to our surrender by answering our prayers and helping us in every way.

Prayer of Application

God, my Father, thank you for your continual workmanship in my life.[1] I fully surrender my life to you, and I know you will meet all my needs according to your riches in glory by Christ Jesus.[2] Thank you, dear God.

Help me to remain rooted and grounded in your Word, Father.[3] I always want to be your steadfast, unmovable worker who always knows that my labor is never in vain in you.[4]

In absolute surrender to your Word and your will, I will run the race you've set before me, ever looking to Jesus, the author and finisher of my faith. For the joy that was set before Him, He endured the cross, despising the shame, and now He is sitting down at your right hand, Father.[5] With great joy I surrender to you, and I thank you for helping me to keep my commitment to you.

Thank you, Father, for your promise that you will not forsake me nor destroy me nor forget the covenant you have made.[6] I believe all of your Word, and I know that not one word of all your good promises has ever failed, and none of your promises ever shall fail.[7] I will always remember your covenant with me,[8] and I will endeavor to obey my part of that covenant with you by keeping my commitment to you in absolute surrender.[9]

You are my God, dear Father, and it is my privilege to ever be your servant.[10] I join myself completely to you, Lord God.[11] Thank you for all that you are doing in my life. I love you so much.

References: (1) *Ephesians 2:10;* (2) *Philippians 4:19;* (3) *Colossians 2:7;* (4) *1 Corinthians 15:58;* (5) *Hebrews 12:1-2;* (6) *Deuteronomy 4:31;* (7) *1 Kings 8:56;* (8) *Hebrews 8:6;* (9) *Jeremiah 11:4;* (10) *Jeremiah 30:22;* (11) *Jeremiah 50:5.*

REMEMBER THIS: **GOD EXPECTS YOUR FULL AND ABSOLUTE SURRENDER. IN RESPONSE, HE PROMISES TO MEET YOUR EVERY NEED.**

11

KEY # 11 – TRUSTING IN THE LORD GOD

Trust in the Lord with all your heart, and lean not on your own understanding; in all your ways acknowledge Him, and He shall direct your paths.
(Prov. 3:5-6, NKJV)

Trust and Faith

There is a close relationship between trust and faith, and both are integral parts of an effective prayer life. Trust is a deep personal confidence in God and His faithfulness. Faith is very similar to trust. Faith is a firm conviction that comes from hearing God's Word. There is a quality inherent in Bible faith that compels one to take action that corresponds with that faith.

As it relates to prayer, trust, therefore, is an unshakable confidence in the promises of God's Word, and in God's willingness and ability to hear and answer prayer. Such trust leads to blessedness: "Blessed is the man who trusts in the Lord, and whose hope is the Lord. For he shall be like a tree planted by the waters, which spreads out its roots by the river, and will not fear when heat comes; but its leaf will be green, and will not be anxious in the year of drought, nor will cease from yielding fruit" (Jer. 17:7-8, NKJV).

Blessedness is the complete happiness that comes to our hearts as we realize that God has everything under control. Trust is the avenue on which those blessings travel in our direction from the heart of God.

E.M. Bounds describes trust as follows: "Trust sees God doing things here and now. Yea, more. It rises to a lofty eminence, and looking into the invisible and the eternal, realizes that God has done things, and regards them as being already done. Trust brings eternity into the annals and happenings of time, transmutes the substance of hope into the reality of fruition, and changes promise into present possession. We know when we trust just as we know when we see, just as we are conscious of the sense of touch. Trust sees, receives, holds. Trust is its own witness."

Trusting Is Resting

Trusting in God is resting in Him. He is infinitely trustworthy, and His promises to us can always be counted on. John Wesley, the founder of Methodism, wrote, "It is a little thing to trust God as far as we can see Him, so far as the way lies open before us; but to trust in Him when we are hedged in on every side and see no way to escape, this is good and acceptable with God."

God is always faithful. "Through the Lord's mercies we are not consumed, because His compassions fail not. They are new every morning; Great is Your faithfulness. 'The Lord is my portion,' says my soul, 'therefore I hope in Him!' The Lord is good to those who wait for Him, to the soul who seeks Him" (Lam. 3:22-25, NKJV).

Faith in the promises of God's Word leads us to trust the great Promise-keeper who always wants only the best for us, His children. Our Father is always near. The knowledge of this truth wipes all fear away. "I will fear no evil: for thou art with me" (Ps. 23:4).

What does God promise to those who trust Him?

"And we know that all things work together for good to them that love God, to them who are the called according to his purpose" (Rom. 8:28).

"Casting all your care upon him; for he careth for you" (1 Pet. 5:7).

"It is better to trust in the Lord than to put confidence in man" (Ps. 118:8).

"He that handleth a matter wisely shall find good: and whoso trusteth in the Lord, happy is he" (Prov. 16:20).

"Every word of God is pure: he is a shield unto them that put their trust in him" (Prov. 30:5).

"Trust in the Lord, and do good; so shalt thou dwell in the land, and verily thou shalt be fed" (Ps. 37:3).

Through prayer we express our trust and confidence in God to Him as we put our petitions before Him in the full expectancy that He will move in our behalf. This is the kind of trust that God always rewards.

Every Promise Fulfilled

Joshua wrote, "Not one of all the Lord's good promises to the house of Israel failed; every one was fulfilled" (Josh. 21:45, NIV). God intends to fulfill every promise He has ever made, and these special promises are for every believer to trust and receive. David prayed, "Those who know your name will trust in you, for you, Lord, have never forsaken those who seek you" (Ps. 9:10, NIV).

When King Solomon dedicated the glorious temple, he reminded the Israelites: "Not one word has failed of all the good promises" (1 Kings 8:56, NIV). Paul, like

Joshua and David, proclaimed, "For all the promises of God in him are yea, and in him Amen, unto the glory of God by us" (2 Cor. 1:20).

God expects us to claim His promises through prayer, and this is an important part of trusting Him.

A.W. Tozer explains the resting nature of trust as follows: "Upon God's faithfulness rests our whole hope of future blessedness. Only as He is faithful will His covenants stand and His promises be honored. Only as we have complete assurance that He is faithful may we live in peace and look forward with assurance to the life to come."

Trusting God Brings Joy

"Let all those that put their trust in thee rejoice: let them ever shout for joy" (Ps. 5:11). The joy that we derive from trusting God has nothing to do with the external circumstances of our life. It comes from deep wellsprings within our souls. It is a never-ending joy. It is rooted in the certain knowledge that God is working His purposes out, no matter what the circumstances may appear to be.

Billy Sunday, the famous evangelist said, "If you have no joy in your religion, there's a leak in your Christianity somewhere." Trust has no leaks, because it comes from unshakable faith. It permits absolutely no doubt to enter in. Trust has complete confidence in God.

The prophet Nehemiah wrote, "The joy of the Lord is your strength" (Neh. 8:10). This abundant joy is grounded in trust. Jesus said, "These things have I spoken unto you, that my joy might remain in you, and that your joy might be full. This is my commandment, That ye love one another, as I have loved you" (John 15:11-12). It is the Word of God, as Jesus points out, that gives us joy and trust. The outgrowth of these qualities is love for God and others.

God Is Utterly Faithful

"Faithful is he that calleth you, who also will do it" (1 Thess. 5:24). Trusting God is having utter confidence in His utter faithfulness. He will do what He promises. He will accomplish great things in your life. He will finish the work He's begun, so that you will be able to say with David, "Thou hast dealt well with thy servant, O Lord, according unto thy word" (Ps. 119:65).

Trusting in God's faithfulness is believing that He is always with you, as the Bible promises: "And, behold, I am with thee, and will keep thee in all places whither thou goest, and will bring thee again into this land; for I will not leave thee, until I have done that which I have spoken to thee of" (Gen. 28:15).

Trusting in God's faithfulness is believing that God loves you. "But because the Lord loved you, and because he would keep the oath which he had sworn unto your fathers, hath the Lord brought you out with a mighty hand, and redeemed you out of the house of bondmen, from the hand of Pharaoh king of Egypt. Know therefore that the Lord thy God, he is God, the faithful God, which keepeth covenant and mercy with them that love him and keep his commandments to a thousand generations" (Deut. 7:8-9).

Trusting in God's faithfulness is believing He will keep His Word. "Ye know in all your hearts and in all your souls, that not one thing hath failed of all the good things which the Lord your God spake concerning you; all are come to pass unto you, and not one thing hath failed thereof" (Josh. 23:14).

Getting Established in Trust

It takes time for trust to develop in a personal relationship. Trusting God develops primarily in two ways. One way is through the study of the Scriptures wherein we see God's faithfulness to others. Also, as we read His Word, faith to trust Him arises in our hearts. Our faith and confidence in God increases and we are encouraged to trust and rely on Him.

The other way our trust in God develops is in our daily interaction with Him. This is one reason why it is important for us to have a daily walk with God. Our constancy in seeking Him daily in everything allows us to personally experience His faithfulness, and our trust in Him grows deeper and fuller.

Through prayer we claim God's faithful promises. As we learn to pray according to His Word He hears us and moves in our behalf. This enables us to proclaim: "I will say of the Lord, He is my refuge and my fortress: my God, in him will I trust. Surely he shall deliver thee from the snare of the fowler, and from the noisome pestilence. He shall cover thee with his feathers, and under his wings shalt thou trust: his truth shall be thy shield and buckler" (Ps. 91:2-4).

Trust establishes our heart in love, not fear. "He shall not be afraid of evil tidings: his heart is fixed, trusting in the Lord. His heart is established, he shall not be afraid, until he see his desire upon his enemies" (Ps. 112:7-8).

Trust leads us to pray the triumphant words of the Psalmist: "Hold up my goings in thy paths, that my footsteps slip not. I have called upon thee, for thou wilt hear me, O

God: incline thine ear unto me, and hear my speech. Shew thy marvellous lovingkindness, O thou that savest by thy right hand them which put their trust in thee from those that rise up against them. Keep me as the apple of thy eye, hide me under the shadow of thy wings" (Ps. 17:5-8).

D. L. Moody wrote, "Just take God at His Word and trust His Son this very day, this very hour, this very moment. . . .to believe on the Lord Jesus Christ is simply to take Him at His Word." Trusting in the Lord, therefore, is taking Him at His Word. "Oh, taste and see that the Lord is good; Blessed is the man who trusts in him!" (Ps. 34:8, NKJV).

Prayer of Application

Heavenly Father, thank you for showing me the power and truth of trust. With your help, I will trust in you with all my heart. Help me not to lean on my own understanding, but in all my ways to acknowledge you. As I do so, Lord God, I know you will direct my paths.[1] Thank you, Father.

My heart is fixed, mighty God. I do trust you with all my possessions and everything in my life. Through trust in you I have no fear.[2] Help me to keep growing in my ability to trust you, Father, because I know that true joy, strength, and blessing come from trusting you fully.[3]

Great is your faithfulness, mighty God. Your mercies to me are new every day.[4] As I trust in you, I commit myself to continuing in supplication and prayer both night and day.[5] Grant that I will never place my trust in uncertain riches, or in any other thing, except you, the living God, who richly gives me all things to enjoy.[6]

How I rejoice in your promise that whoever trusts in you will become like a tree planted by the waters, that spreads out its roots by the river.[7] I want to become such a person by meditating upon your Word, realizing that whatever I do, therefore, will prosper.[8] Thank you, Father. As I learn to trust you, I realize that your mercy is encompassing me.[9]

I now know, mighty God, that all things do indeed work together for good in my life, and will always do so, because I love you and trust you.[10] Hallelujah for this glorious truth!

References: *(1) Proverbs 3:5-6; (2) Psalms 112:7; (3) Proverbs 3:5-6; (4) Lamentations 3:23; (5) 1 Timothy 5:5; (6) 1 Timothy 6:17-18; (7) Jeremiah 17:7-8; (8) Psalms 1; (9) Psalms 32:10-11; (10) Romans 8:28.*

REMEMBER THIS: GOD WANTS YOU TO TRUST HIM WITH ALL YOUR HEART. FULLY TRUSTING HIM, YOU CAN EXPECT HIM TO HEAR AND ANSWER YOUR PRAYERS.

12

KEY # 12 – A FORGIVING HEART

*And whenever you stand praying, if
you have anything against anyone,
forgive him, that your Father in heaven
may also forgive you your trespasses.
But if you do not forgive, neither
will your Father in heaven
forgive your trespasses.*
(Mark 11:25-26, NKJV)

Forgiveness – an Attitude for Prayer

Jesus said, "For if ye forgive men their trespasses, your heavenly Father will also forgive you" (Matt. 6:14). When we harbor any form of unforgiveness in our hearts we stifle the power of our prayers, because the attitude of our hearts is wrong. This is a clear principle in the Word of God. Our Father wants us to have a forgiving heart toward others.

Paul wrote, "Forbearing one another, and forgiving one another, if any man have a quarrel against any: even as Christ forgave you, so also do ye" (Col. 3:13). When we realize how much we've needed forgiveness in our own life (due to our fallen humanity and its propensity for mistakes), we can quickly understand the importance of forgiving others.

John wrote, "If we confess our sins, he is faithful and just to forgive us our sins, and to cleanse us from all unrighteousness" (1 John 1:9). When we sin, we are sinning against God as well as others and ourselves. But our God is faithful, and when we confess our sins He does forgive us and cleanse us from all unrighteousness. We need to forgive others as well, in the same attitude of understanding and mercy that Christ has extended toward us.

Seventy Times Seven

Peter came to Jesus with a question that had obviously been troubling him: "Lord, how oft shall my brother sin against me, and I forgive him? Till seven times? Jesus saith unto him, I say not unto thee, Until seven times: but, Until seventy times seven" (Matt. 18:21-22).

Seven is the number of perfection, and perfection is reemphasized when Jesus says, "Until seventy times seven." 490 times is the Master's symbol for saying that we must keep on forgiving one who sins against us. Indeed, we have no other choice, for we have given ourselves to the forgiving God who shows us the way in all things.

Again, Jesus said, "Take heed to yourselves: If thy brother trespass against thee, rebuke him; and if he repent, forgive him" (Luke 17:3).

What is the connection between a forgiving heart and prayer? Jesus said, "And when ye stand praying, forgive, if ye have ought against any. . ." (Mark 11:25).

Corrie ten Boom, the author of *The Hiding Place* (her autobiographical account of her experiences in a Nazi concentration camp), wrote that after the war she had an experience with forgiveness that totally changed her life. She was speaking in a church in Germany and noticed one of the cruel prison camp guards who had been particularly mean to her and her sister, Betsy, sitting in the congregation. She reported that she felt an intense anger rising within her toward the man.

Inwardly, even while she was speaking, she began to pray, asking God to help her, but every time she looked at the man, the anger surfaced again. She determined to avoid looking at him for the duration of the service. Then she realized that at the conclusion of the service she would be called upon to greet those in attendance as they filed out of the church. This she really did not want to do because she knew her former persecutor would be in the line along with the others.

After the service, just prior to taking her stand at the door to greet the parishioners, she prayed once more. "Father, help me." This was the only prayer she could muster the energy to pray. She was aware of the man getting closer to her as she spoke with the other folks who were leaving.

God spoke to her heart. He told Corrie to forgive the man and to shake his hand. She did not really feel like doing either thing, but willed herself to obey God. She said that as soon as she took his hand in hers, in an act of obedience, it was as if the power of God shot through her body. She was overwhelmed by a realization of God's great love for this man and she was truly able to forgive him. It was then, Corrie later said, that she knew the power of forgiveness and its important role in prayer.

She was reminded of the words of Jesus, "But I say to you, love your enemies, bless those who curse you, do good to those who hate you, and pray for those who spitefully use you and persecute you" (Matt. 5:44, NKJV). When we forgive others, it releases them, and it also releases us to pray and minister more effectively.

Be Reconciled to Each Other

Throughout the gospels the important theme of forgiveness is depicted in a variety of ways. Jesus preached forgiveness wherever He went. We read, "Therefore, if you are offering your gift at the altar and there remember that your brother has something against you, leave your gift there in front of the altar. First go and be reconciled to your brother; then come and offer your gift" (Matt. 5:23-24, NIV).

First things first. Christianity is a bundle of relationships rolled into one neat package. Our relationship with God must always come first. Jesus said, "But seek first the kingdom of God and His righteousness, and all these things shall be added to you" (Matt. 6:33, NKJV). Whatever impedes our relationship with God must be dealt with when we go to Him in prayer; otherwise, our prayer will seem empty and our communication with God will be blocked.

It is equally important for the other relationships of our life to be in order as well. This would include marriage, parenting, family, work, church, and other relationships. If anything is amiss in any of these relationships we need to do what we can to make them right before we go to prayer.

Unforgiveness in our hearts blocks our capacity to love, and love is the keystone of all of our relationships as Christians. This is why Jesus stresses forgiveness over and over again, and He ties it into the life of prayer.

Unforgiveness also stifles the power and the functioning of our faith. Paul told the Galatians that their faith was to work through love. (See Gal. 5:6.) Since love forgives and faith works through love, we can pray the prayer of faith more effectively when our hearts are free from all unforgiveness.

This truth is really quite reasonable when you think about it. The very essence of God's nature is love. He is love and, therefore, all of His gifts and fruit function by love. Our faith is a gift from Him. Therefore, our faith must work through love. This love is also the grace that enables us to forgive others.

Imitators of God

Paul wrote, "And be kind to one another, tenderhearted, forgiving one another, even as God in Christ forgave you. Therefore be imitators of God as dear children. And walk in love" (Eph. 4:32-5:2, NKJV).

Our awesome God is a forgiving God. His Son, our Lord and Savior Jesus Christ, is a forgiving Master. To imitate them we must be forgiving toward others even when they wrong us.

Time after time God was wronged by the people who carried His name, and time after time Jesus was wronged both by believers and unbelievers.

Even so, they forgive freely, and we must do the same.

The model prayer of Jesus – the Lord's Prayer – reveals what the attitudes of our heart should be when we go to God in prayer: "And forgive us our debts, as we forgive our debtors" (Matt. 6:12). When we utter these words, it is advisable for us to remember the clear meaning of what we are praying. Do we really want God to forgive us in the same way we forgive others? If we do, it is imperative for us to be sure that we have forgiven all those who have wronged us. When we fail to do this, we open the door to bitterness and resentment – those twin attitudes that lead to prayerlessness and powerlessness in prayer. It is wise for us to remember that unforgiveness is sin and sin opens the door to the enemy. We close that door through the obedience of forgiveness.

Forbearing and Forgiving

To the Colossians, Paul wrote these words: "Forbearing one another, and forgiving one another, if any man have a quarrel against any: even as Christ forgave you, so also do ye" (Col. 3:13). Forbearing and forgiving are attitudes of the heart, but they are also actions we take toward others.

Forgiving is letting go of all feelings of resentment. It is to pardon, relieve, and overlook the sins of others. It is, insofar as possible, a form of forgetting as well. People often say, "I can forgive, but I can't forget." This is oftentimes true because forgetting is centered in the mind whereas forgiving comes from the heart. We may not be able to eradicate the memory of a wrong, but the more we exercise forgiveness from our hearts the less the memory will be able to dominate our thoughts.

Forbearance, in a similar vein, is the exercise of self-restraint which involves refraining from enforcing something that is due. Forbearance never seeks gratification of feelings of resentment and it does not seek to exact vengeance. It also implies the control of oneself when provoked.

Peter discusses the attitudes of forgiveness and forbearance in one of his letters: "For this is thankworthy, if a man for conscience toward God endure grief, suffering wrongfully. For what glory is it, if, when ye be buffeted for your faults, ye shall take it patiently? But if, when ye do well, and suffer for it, ye take it patiently, this is acceptable with God. For even hereunto were ye called: because Christ also suffered for us, leaving us an example, that ye should follow his steps: Who did no sin, neither was guile found in his mouth: Who, when he was reviled, reviled not again; when he suffered, he threatened not; but committed himself to him that judgeth righteously" (1 Pet. 2:19-23).

The Proactive Response Brings Joy

When someone comes against us in any way we have a choice as to how we will respond. We may react, which usually means that we will try to hurt the individual in the same way they have treated us. We may be inactive, which essentially means we do nothing. Or we may be proactive, which means we take positive steps to bring reconciliation into the situation.

Jesus gives us His model for conflict resolution, "But I say unto you, Love your enemies, bless them that curse you, do good to them that hate you, and pray for them which despitefully use you, and persecute you" (Matt. 5:44). Proactive forgiving and forbearing are acts of love.

Paul echoes this thought in resounding tones: "Be not overcome of evil, but overcome evil with good" (Rom. 12:21).

It seems almost paradoxical, but prayer helps us to forgive, and that's why Jesus asks us to pray for those who persecute us. Not forgiving blocks our prayers because it blocks our ability to love. Therefore, one of the most proactive things we can do is to pray for those who hurt us, attack us or come against us. It is impossible to continue to hate someone we are praying for. As we pray for them it opens the way for God to soften our hearts and this enables us to let forgiveness flow into us and out through us to others.

Prayer of Application

O God, my gracious and forgiving Father, I thank you for your Word which shows me how to conduct my life. It truly is a lamp unto my feet and a light unto my path.[1] You have forgiven me of all my sins, and I praise your holy name.[2] Thank you for removing my transgressions from me as far as the east is from the west.[3] You have always been merciful toward me, and I thank you for choosing to forgive me of my sins.[4] Continue to have mercy upon me, Father. Thank you for your rich and abundant pardon in my life.[5]

Help me to forgive others as you have forgiven me.[6] Through your grace I choose to forgive all those who have wronged me. Enable me, O Lord God, to forbear with them in the same way that Christ has forgiven me.[7] When I stand praying, I will remember to forgive anyone who has come against me, knowing that you will also forgive me.[8] Thank you for the power of forgiveness, Father.

Fill me with your Holy Spirit[9] so that I will walk in love toward others always. Let your love be poured out by your Holy Spirit within my heart[10] so that I will always respond to the actions of others with love and forgiveness. Praise your mighty name, dear Father.

References: (1) Psalms 119:105; (2) Psalms 85:2; (3) Psalms 103:12; (4) Hebrews 8:12; (5) Isaiah 55:7; (6) Matthew 6:12-18; (7) Colossians 3:13; (8) Mark 11:25; (9) Ephesians 5:18; (10) Romans 5:5.

REMEMBER THIS: FORGIVE OTHERS AND GOD WILL FORGIVE YOU. FORGIVENESS IS A GREAT AVENUE OF BLESSING IN YOUR LIFE AND THE LIVES OF OTHERS.

13

KEY # 13 – AGREEMENT IN PRAYER

If two of you agree on earth concerning anything that they ask, it will be done for them by My Father in heaven. For where two or three are gathered together in My name, I am there in the midst of them.
(Matt. 18:19-20, NKJV)

Agreeing With God and His Word

Prevailing prayer, as we have already pointed out, must be in full agreement with the Word of God. The Bible says, "Now this is the confidence that we have in Him, that if we ask anything according to His will, He hears us. And if we know that He hears us, whatever we ask, we know that we have the petitions that we have asked of Him" (1 John 5:14-15, NKJV).

To ask for our petitions according to the will of God is to ask according to His Word. Therefore, it's very appropriate to actually build our prayers from the Bible itself. Jesus said, "If you abide in Me, and My words abide in you, you will ask what you desire, and it shall be done for you" (John 15:7, NKJV).

Praying God's Word, and letting Jesus' words abide in us help us to know the will of God. This assures that God will hear our prayers, and grant our petitions.

Ascertaining the Will of God

The Scriptures provide us with valuable insights into the will of God which help us to know how to pray more effectively. Some of these indications of His will are cited in the following verses:

"If any of you lack wisdom, let him ask of God, that giveth to all men liberally, and upbraideth not; and it shall be given him" (James 1:5).

"For the commandment is a lamp; and the law is light; and reproofs of instruction are the way of life" (Prov. 6:23).

"And thine ears shall hear a word behind thee, saying, This is the way, walk ye in it, when ye turn to the right hand, and when ye turn to the left" (Isa. 30:21).

"Thou gavest also thy good spirit to instruct them, and withheldest not thy manna from their mouth, and gavest them water for their thirst" (Neh. 9:20).

"And the Lord shall guide thee continually, and satisfy thy soul in drought, and make fat thy bones: and thou shalt be like a watered garden, and like a spring of water, whose waters fail not" (Isa. 58:11).

"Howbeit when he, the Spirit of truth, is come, he will guide you into all truth: for he shall not speak of himself; but whatsoever he shall hear, that shall he speak: and he will shew you things to come" (John 16:13).

The preceding selections are but a few biblical references concerning God's will for us. It is His will that we have wisdom, and the way to obtain that wisdom is through prayer. It is His will that we know and follow His commandments, and this process is set into motion through the Word and prayer. It is His will that we learn to discern the voice of God, and this is accomplished through prayer. It is His will that we receive instruction and provision, and these wonderful blessings are imparted through prayer. It is His will that we receive God's guidance, and this comes to us through the Word and prayer. It is His will for us to prosper, and prayer is a great avenue of blessing in our lives. It is His will for us to be led by the Spirit of God who will guide us into all truth, and as we apply His spiritual truths in prayer we receive His guidance in our lives.

Agreeing with God and His Word in prayer results in dynamic, life-changing victory in our prayer life.

Agreement With Other Believers

The prophet Amos wrote, "Can two walk together, unless they are agreed?" (Amos 3:3, NKJV). We all know the answer to this rhetorical question; it is a resounding no. A married couple cannot walk together unless they are in agreement. A pastor and his congregation cannot walk together unless they are in agreement. A strong cement of agreement among people is prayer. Prayer binds us together in ways that go far beyond conversation and activity.

Jesus said, "And if a house be divided against itself, that house cannot stand" (Mark 3:25, NKJV). Agreement is a vital key to answered prayer and spiritual victory.

In spiritual warfare, agreement in prayer among believers is vitally important. Notice what happens in a nation when believers unite in prayerful agreement: "I exhort therefore, that, first of all, supplications, prayers, intercessions, and giving of thanks, be made for all men; for kings, and for all that are in authority; that we may lead a quiet and peaceable life in all godliness and honesty. For this is good and acceptable in the sight of God our Saviour" (1 Tim. 2:1-3).

God promises to answer the prayer of agreement for a nation and its leaders by giving the people peaceable living in all godliness and honesty. This is, in fact, His will for us.

Similarly, we find the divine mandate to pray the prayer of agreement in 2 Chronicles 7:14-15: "If My people who are called by My name will humble themselves, and pray and seek My face, and turn from their wicked ways, then I will hear from heaven, and will forgive their sin and heal their land. Now My eyes will be open and My ears attentive to prayer made in this place" (NKJV). This is a promise to God's people collectively, not to individual believers. It is either all together, or it is not at all.

God promises such agreeing people of prayer: "Blessed is the nation whose God is the Lord; and the people whom he hath chosen for his own inheritance" (Ps. 33:12).

Notice what happened in the early church when the assembled believers agreed in prayer: "So continuing daily with one accord in the temple, and breaking bread from house to house, they ate their food with gladness and simplicity of heart, praising God and having favor with all the people. And the Lord added to the church daily those who were being saved" (Acts 2:46-47, NKJV).

These believers were in one accord when they prayed, and God answered their prayer of agreement by sending new converts into their midst every day. Agreeing prayer, therefore, is a key to church growth in much the same way as it is a key to national peace and security.

Spiritual Warfare

Agreement in prayer is absolutely essential to waging an effective warfare against Satan and his domain. As we agree with God and other believers we are given the opportunity to watch God move in our behalf, as the writer of Second Chronicles shows us: "And he said, Hearken ye, all Judah, and ye inhabitants of Jerusalem, and thou king Jehoshaphat, Thus saith the Lord unto you, Be not afraid nor dismayed by reason of this great multitude; for the battle is not yours, but God's. Tomorrow go ye down against them: behold they come up by the cliff of Ziz; and ye shall find them at the end of the brook, before the wilderness of Jeruel. Ye shall not need to fight in this battle: set yourselves, stand ye still, and see the salvation of the Lord with you, O Judah and Jerusalem: fear not, nor be dismayed: tomorrow go out against them: for the Lord will be with you" (2 Chron. 20:15-17).

Agreement with God and His Word, as well as agreement with other believers, strengthens our faith. We no longer fear the enemy because we know that the battle is God's. He will fight for us. He will go before us. He will be with us. There is an old saying that fear knocked on the door, faith answered, and no one was there.

In warfare, total agreement and unity among the warriors are vitally important. If there is division in any form, the security of the armed forces is greatly threatened. The same is very true in spiritual warfare. This is why Jesus said so emphatically: "That if two of you shall agree on earth as touching any thing that they shall ask, it shall be done for them of my Father which is in heaven. For where two or three are gathered together in my name, there am I in the midst of them" (Matt. 18:19-20).

There is a spiritual dynamic that happens when we pray God's Word in agreement with others. The Scripture tells us that in battle, one of God's people shall be able to chase a thousand of the enemy, and two of God's people fighting together shall be able to put ten thousand to flight. (See Deut. 32:30.)

As we apply this principle of agreement to prayer, Jesus is present with us, and God's power is multiplied. This is one reason why it is good to have a prayer partner to pray with on a regular basis. Many Christian couples have discovered that such agreement in prayer has resulted in many blessings, miracles, and victories.

Agreement, unity, accord – three facets of the same sparkling diamond of truth, a diamond that cannot be shattered because it is stronger than anything else. The Bible puts it this way: "Two are better than one, because they have a good reward for their labor. For if they fall, one will lift up his companion. But woe to him who is alone when he falls, for he has no one to help him up. Again, if two lie down together, they will keep warm; but how can one be warm alone? Though one may be empowered by another, two can withstand him. And a threefold cord is not quickly broken" (Eccles. 4:9-12, NKJV).

The power of unity – being in one accord – is a great key to prevailing power in spiritual warfare as it is a key to answered prayer.

With One Accord

In the Book of Acts we read: "So when they heard that, they raised their voice to God with one accord and said: 'Lord, You are God, who made heaven and earth and the sea, and all that is in them. . . .And when they had prayed, the place where they were assembled together was shaken; and they were all filled with the Holy Spirit, and they spoke the word of God with boldness" (Acts 4:24-31, NKJV). As a result of their praying with one accord, the believers were all filled with the Holy Spirit, and they were empowered to speak the Word of God with a degree of boldness they had never known before.

The passage goes on, "Now the multitude of those who believed were of one heart and one soul; neither did anyone say that any of the things he possessed was his own, but they had all things in common. And with great power the apostles gave witness to the resurrection of the Lord Jesus. And great grace was upon them all" (Acts 4:32-33, NKJV).

The prayer of agreement resulted in the believers having one heart and one soul. They surrendered their rights of ownership. As a result, God gave the apostles great power to witness, and grace fell upon the entire assembly.

Not long thereafter, the Apostle Peter was thrown into prison because of his preaching. The believers who were associated with him stood by him, however, by remaining in an attitude of believing prayer. "Peter was. . . kept in prison, but constant prayer was offered to God for him by the church" (Acts 12:5, NKJV). God heard the united believers' prayer of agreement, sent an angel who set

Peter free, and the apostle was able to rejoice in his new-found freedom, "Now I know for certain that the Lord has sent His angel, and has delivered me from the hand of Herod and from all the expectation of the Jewish people" (Acts 12:11, NKJV).

When Peter arrived at the house of Mary, the mother of John Mark, what did he find? ". . . many were gathered together praying" (Acts 12:12, NKJV). It is clear that being of one heart and one soul led the early believers to continually pray the prayer of agreement – a prayer that God heard and honored on numerous occasions just as He does today.

The Unity of All Believers

Individual prayer is important, and so is solitude. However, uniting with other believers is vitally important as well. We are parts of each other, "And whether one member suffer, all the members suffer with it; or one member be honoured, all the members rejoice with it. Now ye are the body of Christ, and members in particular" (1 Cor. 12:26-27).

The reality of the Body of Christ – the Church – is what impels Peter to write these words: "Finally, be ye all of one mind, having compassion one of another, love as brethren, be pitiful, be courteous: not rendering evil for evil, or railing for railing: but contrariwise blessing; knowing that ye are thereunto called, that ye should inherit a blessing" (1 Pet. 3:8-9).

Jesus clarifies this concept of unity for us: "For where two or three are gathered together in my name, there am I in the midst of them" (Matt. 18:20). When we gather in the name of Jesus, He is present to hear our prayers and minister to our needs .

Paul reminds us: "God is faithful, by whom ye were called unto the fellowship of his Son Jesus Christ our Lord. Now I beseech you, brethren, by the name of our Lord Jesus Christ, that ye all speak the same thing, and that there be no divisions among you; but that ye be perfectly joined together in the same mind and in the same judgment" (1 Cor. 1:9-10).

E.M. Bounds writes: "In the Church, however, God is acknowledged, and nothing is done without Him. Prayer is the one distinguishing mark of the house of God. As prayer distinguishes Christian from unchristian people, so prayer distinguishes God's house from all other houses. It is a place where faithful believers meet with their Lord."

Let us conclude this chapter in full agreement with the prayer of Jesus: "Neither do I pray for these alone, but for them also which shall believe on me through their word; that they all may be one; as thou, Father, art in me, and I in thee, that they also may be one in us: that the world may believe that thou hast sent me. And the glory which thou gavest me I have given them; that they may be one, even as we are one: I in them, and thou in me, that they may be made perfect in one; and that the world may know that thou hast sent me, and hast loved them, as thou hast loved me" (John 17:20-23).

God is fulfilling this prayer in answer to His Son, Jesus. It is a prayer of agreement that will result in perfect unity among believers. Imagine the power that will be exhibited by the Church of Jesus Christ when we become one with Jesus, the Father, and each other in the same way that Jesus is one with the Father.

Prayer of Application

Father, thank you for the prayer of Jesus which asks you to make us all one as you and He are one. I ask you for the continued fulfillment of that prayer so that the world will believe that you have sent Jesus to be both Savior and Lord.[1] Reunite the Body of Christ, Lord God, so that we can experience the blessings you've promised to those who walk together.[2] Help us to learn how to pray the prayer of agreement which will bring your mighty hand to work in our behalf.[3]

Give me grace in every situation to work toward unity with other believers. It is my desire, dear Father, with all lowliness, meekness, and patience to forbear with other believers in love, always endeavoring to keep the unity of the Spirit in the bond of peace,[4] till we all come in the unity of the faith, and of the knowledge of your Son, unto a perfect man, unto the measure of the stature of the fullness of Christ.[5]

Enable your Church to fulfill your joy by becoming like-minded, having the same love, being of one accord, of one mind,[6] as we worship and pray together. Pour forth your Holy Spirit upon us, Father, and give us your grace.[7]

Teach me and my fellow-believers to always pray in agreement with your Word, and in agreement with one another.[8] Help us to wage spiritual warfare through the prayer of agreement,[9] in the name of Jesus Christ.[10]

References: (1) John 17:21; (2) Psalms 133:1-3; (3) Matthew 18:19-20; (4) Ephesians 4:2-6; (5) Ephesians 4:13; (6) Philippians 2:2; (7) Acts 2:1; (8) Matthew 18:19-20; (9) Matthew 18:20; (10) John 16:24.

REMEMBER THIS: **LET US BE SURE TO AGREE WITH ONE ANOTHER AS WE PRAY IN AGREEMENT WITH GOD'S WORD AND WILL. SUCH PRAYING WILL ALWAYS BRING POSITIVE RESULTS!**

14

KEY # 14 – BIBLE MEDITATION

*This Book of the Law shall not depart
from your mouth, but you shall
meditate in it day and night, that
you may observe to do according to
all that is written in it. For then you
will make your way prosperous, and
then you will have good success.*
(Josh. 1:8, NKJV)

The Power of God's Word

As we learn to meditate upon the Word of
God, and let its principles be incorporated into
our prayer life, amazing things begin to
happen. Joshua explains that when we
meditate upon the Bible we learn to follow its
directives, including its instructions concerning prayer. This, according to Joshua, assures
that we will have good success. (See the
epigram above, from Josh. 1:8.)

The same theme is covered in Psalms 1:
"Blessed is the man that walketh not in the
counsel of the ungodly, nor standeth in the
way of sinners, nor sitteth in the seat of the
scornful. But his delight is in the law of the
Lord; and in his law doth he meditate day and
night. And he shall be like a tree planted by the

rivers of water, that bringeth forth his fruit in his season; his leaf also shall not wither; and whatsoever he doeth shall prosper" (Ps. 1:1-3).

Without doubt, therefore, stunning things happen when we learn to meditate upon God's Word. Our success is assured, we will be fruitful, and whatever we do shall prosper. Amazing promises these are, but they are truly God's gift to those who love and revere His Word and walk in its precepts.

For more information on Bible meditation and praying God's Word, refer to the following books that have been published by Victory House, Inc: *Believers' Prayers and Promises*, *Bible Prayers for All Your Needs*, *Praying God's Promises*, *Prayers That Prevail*, *More Prayers That Prevail*, *Prayers That Prevail for Your Children*, *Mini Prayers That Prevail*, and *Breakthrough Prayers for Women*.

Praying the Word

Meditating on God's Word and walking in His Word are very closely related. It seems almost impossible to do one without the other. As we learn to meditate on God's Word, we begin to learn to walk according to its precepts. This leads us to pray in the Word as well, and all three activities serve to build our faith, as Paul pointed out: "So then faith cometh by hearing, and hearing by the word of God" (Rom. 10:17).

Jeremiah said that he ate the words of God. They were the bread of life to him. He wrote, "Thy words were found, and I did eat them; and thy word was unto me the joy and rejoicing of mine heart: for I am called by thy name, O Lord God of hosts" (Jer. 15:16). This is true meditation upon the Word – chewing upon its truths, swallowing them, and letting them become a part of our life. Indeed, God's Word is life and health to every believer.

R.A. Torrey describes praying the Word this way: "We go into God's presence with the thing we desire. Next, we ask ourselves this question: Is there any promise in God's Word regarding what we desire? We look into the Word of God and find the promise. Then all we have to do is to present that promise to God. For example, we say, 'Heavenly Father, we desire the Holy Spirit. You say in your Word, "If ye then, being evil, know how to give good gifts unto your children, how much more shall your heavenly Father give the Holy Spirit to them that ask him?" And again in Acts 2:39, that "the promise is unto you, and to your children, and to all that are afar off, even as many as the Lord our God shall call." I have been called; I am saved; and here in Your Word is Your promise. So please fill me now with the Holy Spirit.'

"We then take 1 John 5:14-15, and say, 'Father, this is the confidence I have in You, that, if I ask anything according to Your will – and know that this is according to Your will – You hear me, and, if I know that You hear me, I know that I have the petition that I have asked of You.' Then we stand on God's promise and say, 'It is mine,' and it will be. The only way to have a faith that prevails in prayer is to study your Bible, know the promises, and present them to God when you pray."

So, then, how do we pray God's Word? We begin by studying the Bible, as Paul advises Timothy: "Be diligent to present yourself approved to God, a worker who does not need to be ashamed, rightly dividing the word of truth" (2 Tim. 2:15, NKJV). This causes faith to arise in our hearts.

In genuine faith, therefore, we are able to believe and receive the promises of God's Word as we pray. This is prevailing prayer. Find God's promises. Study God's promises. Stand upon God's promises. Believe God's promises. Receive God's promises. Live God's promises, and pray God's promises.

Praying the Word of God enables us to receive the answers to our prayer (in the form of His promises) while we are praying.

The Bible says, "My son, attend to my words; incline thine ear unto my sayings. Let them not depart from thine eyes; keep them in the midst of thine heart. For they are life unto those that find them, and health to all their flesh. Keep thy heart with all diligence; for out of it are the issues of life" (Prov. 4:20-23).

Inclining our ear to God's Word, and letting it find its place of residence in our heart, is a great key to effective praying. God's Word is life and health in prayer as in all else.

Jesus said, "If ye abide in me, and my words abide in you, ye shall ask what ye will, and it shall be done unto you" (John 15:7).

Preparation for Prayer

Meditating upon God's Word prepares our heart for prayer and for receiving all that God has in store for us. David prayed, "Give ear to my words, O Lord, consider my meditation. Hearken unto the voice of my cry, my King, and my God: for unto thee will I pray. My voice shalt thou hear in the morning, O Lord; in the morning will I direct my prayer unto thee, and will look up" (Ps. 5:1-3).

This passage shows us the vital link between Bible meditation and prayer which David discovered as a youth.

At another time, David prayed, "Let the words of my mouth, and the meditation of my heart, be acceptable in thy sight, O Lord, my strength, and my redeemer" (Ps. 19:14).

Like David, as we meditate on God's Word, our hearts are prepared to meet with Him, to believe that He hears us, and to receive all that He has in store for us. Prayer thus inspired by our meditation on God's Word is fueled by faith imparted from the Word, and we draw close to our heavenly Father in communion and fellowship in prayer.

The Psalms literally abound with prayers which reveal the important relationship between Bible meditation and prayer:

"My mouth shall speak of wisdom; and the meditation of my heart shall be of understanding" (Ps. 49:3).

"O how I love thy law! It is my meditation all the day. Thou through thy commandments hast made me wiser than mine enemies: for they are ever with me. I have more understanding than all my teachers: for thy testimonies are my meditation" (Ps. 119:97-99).

"I will sing unto the Lord as long as I live: I will sing praise to my God while I have my being. My meditation of him shall be sweet: I will be glad in the Lord" (Ps. 104:33-34).

"My hands also will I lift up unto thy commandments, which I have loved; and I will meditate in thy statutes" (Ps. 119:48).

"I remember the days of old; I meditate on all thy works; I muse on the work of thy hand" (Ps. 143:5).

"When I remember thee upon my bed, and meditate on thee in the night watches. Because thou hast been my help, therefore in the shadow of thy wings will I rejoice. My soul followeth hard after thee: thy right hand upholdeth me" (Ps. 63:6-8).

"Let thy tender mercies come unto me, that I may live: for thy law is my delight. Let the proud be ashamed; for they dealt perversely with me without a cause: but I will meditate in thy precepts" (Ps. 119:77-78).

"I will meditate in thy precepts, and have respect unto thy ways. I will delight myself in thy statutes: I will not forget thy word" (Ps. 119:15-16).

"Thy testimonies also are my delight and my counselors. My soul cleaveth unto the dust: quicken thou me according to thy word" (Ps. 119:24-25).

E.M. Bounds writes, "The Word of God is a great help in prayer. If it be lodged and written in our hearts, it will form an outflowing current of prayer, full and irresistible. Promises, stored in the heart, are to be the fuel from which prayer receives life and warmth, just as the coal, stored in the earth, ministers to our comfort on stormy days and wintry nights. The Word of God is the food, by which prayer is nourished and made strong. Prayer, like man, cannot live by bread alone, 'but by every word which proceedeth out of the mouth of the Lord.'

"Unless the vital forces of prayer are supplied by God's Word, prayer, though earnest, even vociferous, in its urgency, is in reality, flabby, and vapid, and void. The absence of vital force in praying, can be traced to the absence of a constant supply of God's Word, to repair the waste, and renew the life. He who would learn to pray well, must first study God's Word, and store it in his memory and thought."

The Authority of God's Word

By studying and meditating upon the Word of God we learn that it is the voice of ultimate authority because it was inspired by Almighty God. Paul wrote, "All scripture is given by inspiration of God, and is profitable for doctrine, for reproof, for correction, for instruction in righteousness" (2 Tim. 3:16). We know, therefore, that it is our authoritative source for prayer as well.

Andrew Murray wrote, "Little of the Word with little prayer is death to the spiritual life. Much of the Word with little prayer gives a sickly life. Much prayer with little of the Word gives more life, but without steadfastness. A full measure of the Word and prayer each day gives a healthy and powerful life."

This is because God's Word is so powerful, and it makes our prayers powerful as well. "For the word of God is quick, and powerful, and sharper than any two-edged sword, piercing even to the dividing asunder of soul and spirit, and of the joints and marrow, and is a discerner of the thoughts and intents of the heart" (Heb. 4:12). Indeed, the Bible is a mirror which reveals our true motives in prayer.

God's Word will never return unto Him void when it is prayed in full sincerity. "For as the rain cometh down, and the snow from heaven, and returneth not thither, but watereth the earth, and maketh it bring forth and bud, that it may give seed to the sower, and bread to the eater: So shall my word be that goeth forth out of my mouth: it shall not return unto me void, but it shall accomplish that which I please, and it shall prosper in the thing whereto I sent it" (Isa. 55:10-11).

Jack Hayford writes, "Few things have contributed to spiritual barrenness in the church Christ founded as has the idea that prayer is mere quiet, meditational passivism.

"There is a time to be silent. There is a time to be still. To know the awesomeness of God's person and presence. But prayer is alive. It is aloud with praise, aglow with warmth, attuned with song, aflame with power. And it is also unsettling in its violence. Not in the violence of its practice, but in the violence of its impact when it is exercised in power."

Nothing allows us to exercise power in prayer more than meditating upon God's powerful Word and letting its mighty authority ring with every word we pray.

Prayer of Application

God, I come to you now in complete thankfulness for your Word which truly is a lamp unto my feet and a light unto my path.[1] With your help, Father, I will walk in the precepts of your Word,[2] I will mediate upon its principles,[3] and I will pray its promises.[4] Thank you for increasing my faith as I meditate upon your Word and pray according to its truth.[5]

Thank you for inspiring your Word, Father, so that I might be fully furnished with good works, including prayer.[6] As I study your Word you show me how to rightly divide its truth[7] which has made me free.[8]

By meditating on your Word as I pray, Lord God, you have granted me good success[9] in every area of my life. You are establishing me like a tree that is planted by the rivers of water, and you are making me fruitful in every area of my life and ministry.[10] Thank you, Father, for showing me that as I take heed to your Word you are able to prosper me.[11] I choose to meditate upon your powerful Word, and as I do so, I know you will never let it return unto you void. Thank you for your promise to have your Word accomplish your purposes in my life.[12]

I praise you for your Word, dear Father, and I take it as the sword of your Spirit, knowing you will enable me to conquer every enemy through its power.[13]

References: (1) Psalms 119:105; (2) Psalms 119:24; (3) Psalms 1; (4) 2 Peter 1:4-8; (5) Romans 10:17; (6) 2 Timothy 3:16-17; (7) 2 Timothy 2:15; (8) John 8:32; (9) Joshua 1:8; (10) Psalms 1; (11) Psalms 1:3; (12) Isaiah 55:10-11; (13) Ephesians 6:17-18.

REMEMBER THIS: **BIBLE MEDITATION WILL MAKE YOU FRUITFUL IN PRAYER AND IN ALL AREAS OF YOUR LIFE. IT WILL BRING YOU GOOD SUCCESS IN ALL YOUR ENDEAVORS.**

15

KEY # 15 – ACTIVE LISTENING

My sheep hear my voice, and I know
them, and they follow me: And I give
unto them eternal life; and
they shall never perish.
(John 10:27-28)

Prayer Is a Dialogue

God created us to have fellowship with Him. Such fellowship takes place through prayer, worship, Bible study, meditation, and communion with other believers. It is the most vital relationship in our lives.

Often problems in relationships occur because of poor communication. In such cases it is frequently true that at least one individual may be a poor listener. Such folks may talk freely, but rarely take the time to listen to what the other person has to say.

Listening is a skillful art that must be learned; it may not come naturally to many people. Active listening is a great bridge of understanding between two or more people. In our relationship with God it is clear that He is a good listener, as the following verses attest:

"He did hear my voice out of his temple, and my cry did enter into his ears" (2 Sam. 22:7).

"Hear thou in heaven thy dwelling place: and when thou hearest, forgive" (1 Kings 8:30).

"I have heard thy prayer, I have seen thy tears: behold, I will heal thee" (2 Kings 20:5).

"He heareth the cry of the afflicted" (Job 34:28).

"The Lord will hear when I call unto him" (Ps. 4:3).

"He forgetteth not the cry of the humble" (Ps. 9:12).

"Blessed be the Lord, because he hath heard the voice of my supplications" (Ps. 28:6).

"I sought the Lord, and he heard me, and delivered me from all my fears" (Ps. 34:4).

"The righteous cry, and the Lord heareth" (Ps. 34:17).

"He shall call upon me, and I will answer him: I will be with him in trouble" (Ps. 91:15).

"The Lord is nigh unto all them that call upon him, to all that call upon him in truth" (Ps. 145:18).

"Call unto me, and I will answer thee" (Jer. 33:3).

"They shall call on my name, and I will hear them" (Zech. 13:9).

God actively listens for our prayers, and He promises to hear us and answer us, but He also wants us to listen to Him. He wants us to learn to discern His voice. As we learn to listen for God, He will guide us, give us His wisdom, show us His ways, and reveal His truth to us.

Personal prayer at its best, then, is a dialogue in which we actively engage in both talking to God and listening to Him. God can speak to us in a variety of ways: through His Word, through circumstances, through His "still, small voice," through our consciences, through nature, through other people, through Christian literature, through worship, and through many other means. He is speaking, and we do need to listen.

Prayer is not meant to be just a one-sided conversation in which we talk to God and hear nothing from Him. Many prayers we hear may seem like sermons, and some even like shopping lists. Others are more like gossip columns in a newspaper. Still others are eloquent speeches and theological discourses.

God desires so much more than that for us. True prayer stems from an intimate, personal relationship with the Father. He wants us to draw close to Him, to get to know Him and His ways, and to listen for His voice.

Prayer is one of the avenues that enables us to know God intimately.

God wants us to call out to Him, to even cry to Him if need be, but He also wants us to learn to recognize His voice speaking to us. Jesus said, "My sheep hear my voice, and I know them, and they follow me: And I give unto them eternal life; and they shall never perish" (John 10:27-28).

Isaiah, the prophet, gives us a clear picture of what can happen when we listen actively for the voice of God: "Your ears shall hear a word behind you, saying, 'This is the way, walk in it'" (Isa. 30:21, NKJV). Such personal words from God dispel all confusion, and they give us certain answers to our prayers.

Through Listening We Get to Know Him

There is a vast difference between knowing about God and actually knowing Him. Jesus gives us the story of Mary and Martha in order to help us understand this difference.

Jesus paid a visit to the two sisters, Mary and Martha. Mary responded to His visit by sitting at His feet and hearing His word while Martha ". . .was cumbered about much serving, and came to him, and said, Lord, dost thou not care that my sister hath left me to serve alone? Bid her therefore that she help me" (Luke 10:40).

Mary knew how to listen to Jesus. Her sister, Martha, on the other hand, was too busy to take the time to listen. Martha knew how to serve the Master, but she did not stop to listen to Him. There was a tinge of jealousy in her voice when she asked Jesus to have Mary help her with the preparations, but Jesus rebuked her, "Martha, Martha, you are worried and troubled about many things. But one thing is needed, and Mary has chosen that good part, which will not be taken away from her" (Luke 10:41-42, NKJV).

What is "that good part" to which Jesus refers? It is the act of worshipful listening at the Master's footstool where each of us learns to discern the voice of God. He will speak to the hearts of those who love Him and want to heed His voice above all others.

God commands us to take the time to listen to Him: "Incline your ear, and come unto me: hear, and your soul shall live; and I will make an everlasting covenant with you, even the sure mercies of David" (Isa. 55:3).

A young lady was a senior in high school when her pastor asked her to sing a solo in church on the Sunday prior to her graduation. Thrilled at this opportunity, the student invited her parents who never attended church to be there to hear her sing.

She was sitting in the front of the congregation when she heard a commotion at the back. Her parents had decided to attend, but both of them were drunk and boisterous! She noticed that they even tripped over people as they tried to take seats in an already-packed pew! Her father even fell into a lady's lap!

The girl hung her head in shame and embarrassment. Then she was called upon to sing. As she ascended the platform, she felt awkward and uncertain. Standing before the congregation, she looked at a stained-glass window that showed Jesus holding a child's hand. She felt she was that child, and God was holding her hand.

She sensed that God was speaking to her, saying, *"I am your Father. I am with you. Just do your best, and I'll do the rest."* Her confidence was restored. She had prayed, and God had answered in His still, small voice. Through active listening, she had learned that all that really matters is her relationship with God, and she sang as she never had before.

The congregation applauded her vigorously, and the pastor said, "God has given you a great gift, young lady. Keep up the good work."

In her heart, she could hear God saying, *"You are My child. I will always be with you."*

God's Glory

To truly listen to God we must quiet our hearts and minds in His presence. In such a peaceful atmosphere we see our awesome God in all His glory. A single glimpse of His glory causes us to remain quiet in His presence, to listen reverently for His voice.

"Be still, and know that I am God: I will be exalted among the heathen, I will be exalted in the earth. The Lord of hosts is with us; the God of Jacob is our refuge" (Ps. 46:10-11).

The implication of this verse is that knowing God comes through quiet listening. The more we listen for Him the more we realize this truth: "Great is the glory of the Lord" (Ps. 138:5).

God's Greatness

The Psalmist writes, "Great is the Lord, and greatly to be praised" (Ps. 48:1). We worship God because His greatness stirs us to cry out to Him. The realization of His greatness causes us to fall on our face in His glorious presence, to honor Him as the elders in the Revelation do before His throne: "Thou art worthy, O Lord, to receive glory and honour and power: for thou hast created all things, and for thy pleasure they were created" (Rev. 4:11).

This view of God's greatness has a tremendous impact upon our prayer life. It leads us to understand that God ". . .is able to do exceeding abundantly above all that we ask or think, according to the power that worketh in us" (Eph. 3:20). Our awesome God is able to accomplish all things.

God's Love

By listening to God we learn how much He loves us, leading us to proclaim with the Psalmist: "Thy lovingkindness is better than life" (Ps. 63:3). We discover that we are "the apple of his eye" (Deut. 32:10). Such knowledge is profoundly wonderful because it changes the way we see God, ourselves, and others. It even changes the way we see the world and its people.

"God is love" (1 John 4:8), and this fact makes all the difference in our lives. It causes us to love others. "If God so loved us, we ought also to love one another" (1 John 4:11).

It removes our fear. "Perfect love casteth out fear" (1 John 4:18).

It leads us into a loving relationship with our heavenly Father. "We love him, because he first loved us" (1 John 4:19).

It enables us to walk in love wherever we go. "Walk in love, as Christ also hath loved us" (Eph. 5:2).

The power of God's love motivates us to listen to His voice and to pray with greater fervency.

God's Presence

God said, "I will dwell in them and walk among them. I will be their God, and they shall be My people" (2 Cor. 6:16, NKJV). In order to listen for the voice of our God we must live in His presence. In Deuteronomy we read: "We have seen this day that God doth talk with man, and he liveth" (Deut. 5:24). God wants to talk with us, and we need to listen for His voice as we abide in His presence day by day and minute by minute.

For these reasons we must seek Him and listen for Him. "That they should seek the Lord, if haply they might feel after him, and find him, though he be not far from every one of us: For in him we live, and move, and have our being; as certain also of your own poets have said, For we are also his offspring" (Acts 17:27-28).

Joshua wrote, "The Lord thy God is with thee whithersoever thou goest" (Josh. 1:9). He promises, "I will never leave thee, nor forsake thee" (Heb. 13:5).

God is with us, and He is speaking to us. In fact, He says, "Mine eyes and mine heart shall be there perpetually" (1 Kings 9:3).

The reality is that "The Lord is nigh unto all them that call upon him in truth" (Ps. 145:18). Jesus said, "Thy Father which seeth in secret shall reward thee openly" (Matt. 6:6). He also proclaimed, "Where two or three are gathered together in my name, there am I in the midst of them" (Matt. 18:20).

As we stay in God's presence we hear His voice speaking to us, and this helps us to know that He will answer our prayers. "And the Lord shall guide thee continually, and satisfy thy soul in drought, and make fat thy bones: and thou shalt be like a watered garden, and like a spring of water, whose waters fail not" (Isa. 58:11).

God promises, "I will instruct thee and teach thee in the way which thou shalt go: I will guide thee with mine eye" (Ps. 32:8)

The Voice of God

Through active listening we become acquainted with the voice of God as Adam and Eve did in the Garden of Eden. (See Gen. 3:8.) God wants us to hearken to His voice. (See Exod. 3:18.) He wants us to obey His voice: "When thou art in tribulation, and all these things are come upon thee, even in the latter days, if thou turn to the Lord thy God, and shalt be obedient unto his voice; (For the Lord thy God is a merciful God;) he will not forsake thee, neither destroy thee, nor forget the covenant of thy fathers which he sware unto them" (Deut. 4:30-31).

The Psalmist describes the voice of the Lord God for us: "The voice of the Lord is upon the waters: the God of glory thundereth: the Lord is upon many waters. The voice of the Lord is powerful; the voice of the Lord is full of majesty" (Ps. 29:3-4). David concludes this passage by writing: "The Lord will give strength unto his people; the Lord will bless his people with peace" (Ps. 29:11).

God's voice is powerful and filled with majesty. We immediately recognize His authority when we hear His voice. What is God's promise to us when we obey His voice? "But this thing commanded I them, saying, Obey my voice, and I will be your God, and ye shall be my people: and walk ye in all the ways that I have commanded you, that it may be well unto you" (Jer. 7:23). Active listening involves hearing His voice and acting upon it.

God's voice is recorded in nearly every book of the Bible. He spoke to the patriarchs, the prophets, and the apostles, and He wants to speak to us as well. Prayer opens our ears to the voice of the Almighty, and He tells us what we need to hear. By listening for His voice we often hear the answers to our prayers.

How do we hear what God is saying? Most often it is an impression, a knowing, or a small voice within our hearts. For the Prophet Elijah, it was a "still small voice" (1 Kings 19:12). Jesus said, "My sheep hear My voice, and I know them, and they follow Me" (John 10:27, NKJV).

As you learn to actively listen for the voice of God, you will want to keep a daily journal of the specific things you wish to say to God and of His answers when they come.

Many Christians have said that keeping a daily prayer journal provides them with a record of their developing relationship with God. Each journal entry should include a record of your prayer requests and questions for God, along with a space for recording His specific answers when they come.

Stick with it, and don't give up even if you don't receive the response you expect right away. You have now entered into God's arena of intimacy, and if you will be patient, He will guide you into fullness of love and friendship with Him.

Prayer of Application

O God, I thank you for the certainty that you know my voice,[1] and you hear my prayers.[2] It is my desire to learn to recognize your voice when you speak to me as well.[3]

With my whole heart I seek you, Father.[4] I know that I will hear your voice speaking to me, and I know I will surely find you.[5] Help me to obey your voice at all times.[6] Thank you for the promise that assures me that when I draw near to you, you will draw near to me.[7] I claim that promise now as I pray.

You are my God, and I will seek you early. My soul thirsts for you. I desire to experience your power and glory. Your lovingkindness is better than life to me. Therefore, my lips shall praise you, and I will bless you.[8] I will also take time to listen for your voice.

You have revealed so many things to me by your Spirit, O God. Mighty things, which I could not have known apart from seeking you, listening for your voice, and waiting on you. Thank you for revealing these things to me, Father. It is so wonderful to know you and to learn your ways.[9]

How I rejoice in the knowledge that you are my Rewarder. Therefore, I come to you in faith, Father, fully believing in you and your desire to speak to me.[10] Thank you for coming to me and speaking to me as I wait in your presence.[11]

References: *(1) John 10:27-28; (2) Jeremiah 33:3; (3) Isaiah 30:21; (4) Deuteronomy 4:29; (5) Psalms 63:1-4; (6) Deuteronomy 4:31-36; (7) James 4:8; (8) Psalms 63:1-4; (9) Jeremiah 33:3; (10) Hebrews 11:6; (11) Psalms 27:14.*

REMEMBER THIS: **GOD IS SPEAKING. ARE YOU LISTENING?**